ated)# 2025 IGE Distinguished Lecture Forum

한국의 국제 신인도 제고와 국가 경쟁력 강화를 위한 전략: 금융의 역할

초판 1쇄 발행 2025년 5월

펴낸이 전광우
지 원 김경진, 김시연
디자인 김정진
인 쇄 한진기획인쇄

펴낸곳 세계경제연구원
전 화 02-551-3334~8
팩 스 02-551-3339
등 록 서울시 강남구 영동대로 511

종이책 ISBN 979-11-6177-051-2 [03320]

종이책 정가 15,000원

*이 책은 저작권법에 따라 보호받는 저작물이므로 무단 전재와 복제를 금합니다.
*잘못된 책은 구입하신 서점에서 바꾸어 드립니다.

2025 IGE Distinguished Lecture Forum

한국의 국제 신인도 제고와 국가 경쟁력 강화를 위한 전략: 금융의 역할

Michael Mainelli

개회사

전광우 세계경제연구원 이사장

존경하는 내외 귀빈 여러분,

오늘 IGE 특별 포럼에 함께해 주신 여러분을 진심으로 환영합니다. 이 자리에 함께해 주신 모든 분들께 깊은 감사와 경의를 표합니다.

오늘 우리는, 트럼프 전 대통령의 재집권이라는 중대한 변화로 상징되는 새로운 국제질서의 전환기에 서 있습니다. 급변하는 글로벌 지정학 환경 속에서, 오늘 포럼의 개최는 그 어느 때보다 시의적절하며 큰 의미를 지닌다고 하겠습니다.

대한민국은 오랜 시간 동안 선제적 정책과 개방적 혁신을 통해 기술, 제조, 국제무역 등 여러 분야에서 세계를 선도하는 국가로 자리매김해 왔습니다. 그러나 우리는 잘 알고 있습니다. 국내외 위기는 언제나 국가의 신뢰와 경쟁력을 시험하는 계기가 되어 왔으며, 이를 슬기롭게 극복하는 능력이야말로 지속 가능한 성장의 핵심 동력이라는 사실을 말입니다.

이에 오늘 우리는 세계 금융과 정책 분야의 탁월한 전문가인 마이클 마이넬리 박사님을 모시게 되었습니다.

마이넬리 박사님은 2023-2024년 런던 시장을 지내셨으며, 현재는 영국 런던 상공회의소 회장을 맡고 계십니다. 뿐만 아니라 국제금융센터지수(GFCI)를 발표하는 Z/Yen 그룹의 설립자이자 회장이시며, 다양한 요직을 두루 거치며 글로벌 경제와 금융의 흐름을 이끌어오신 분입니다. 오늘 이 자리를 통해 박사님께서 들려주실 고견은 우리가 당면한 불확실성과 변화 속에서 새로운 방향을 모색하는 데 큰 통찰을 제공해 줄 것으로 기대합니다.

이 자리를 더욱 뜻깊게 빛내 주신 분들께도 감사의 마음을 전합니다. 먼저, 축사를 보내주신 정운찬 전 국무총리님과 오세훈 서울시장님께 깊은 감사의 말씀을 드립니다. 또한, 오늘 포럼의 성공적인 개최를 위해 지속적인 성원과 후원을 아끼지 않으신 성기학 영원무역 회장님께도 각별한 감사를 드립니다.

존경하는 내외 귀빈 여러분, 오늘 이 자리가 대한민국이 직면한 새로운 시대적 도전을 슬기롭게 극복하고, 국제 사회에서의 위상과 경쟁력을 한층 더 높이는 데 기여하는 귀중한 이정표가 되기를 기대합니다. 참석해 주신 모든 분들께 다시 한 번 감사드립니다.

감사합니다.

축사

정운찬 동반성장연구소 이사장/前 국무총리/前 서울대 총장

존경하는 마이클 마이넬리 특별연사님, 전광우 이사장님, 그리고 귀빈 여러분, 오늘 이 뜻깊은 자리에 참석해 주셔서 진심으로 감사드립니다.

특히, 한국이 많은 어려움에 처해있는 이 때에 특별히 서울을 방문해 주신 마이넬리 회장님께 깊은 감사의 말씀을 드리고 싶습니다. 회장님께서 오늘 이 자리에서 나누어 주실 통찰과 경험은 한국과 국제 사회 간의 중요한 가교 역할을 할 것입니다. 또한 한국이 작금의 경제적 정치적 위기를 극복하고 동아시아의 금융 및 경제 중심지로 더욱 굳건히 자리매김할 수 있는 핵심적 논의를 이끌어 주실 것이라고 기대합니다.

오늘 포럼 주제인 '한국의 국제 신인도 제고와 국가 경쟁력 강화를 위한 전략'은 시의적절하면서 매우 중요한 주제입니다. 한국은 현재 다양한 도전적 상황 속에 있습니다. 저성장과 양극화가 이어지는 한편으로 대내 정치적 불확실성과 트럼프 2기 행정부의 정책 변화, 여러 지정학적 위험 등이 복합적으로 한국 경제에 영향을 미치고 있는 이 시점에서 우리는 이 위기를 기회로 전환해야 할 책임이 있습니다.

이를 위해서는 첫째, 한국의 글로벌 금융 중심지로서 입지와 역할을 더욱 강화해야 합니다. 한국 그 중에서도 서울은 아시아

의 중요한 금융 중심지로, 글로벌 금융 시장에서 중요한 역할을 할 수 있는 충분한 잠재력을 가지고 있습니다. 위기 속에서도 한국의 금융시장은 더욱 개방적이고 혁신적인 방향으로 변화해야 합니다. 그리하여 한국의 주요 산업과 연관 산업의 시너지를 더욱 극대화하고 어려움 속에서도 흔들림 없이 한국의 국제적 리더십과 신뢰를 제고하여 지속가능한 성장을 위한 튼튼한 발판을 마련해야합니다.

둘째, 한국 기업들의 적극적인 해외 진출뿐만 아니라, 글로벌 투자자들의 한국 투자 확대가 필요합니다. 오늘 이 자리에 함께한 금융업계와 기업 그리고 무엇보다 정부의 역할이 중요합니다. 우리는 한국 기업들이 해외로 진출하는 것은 물론, 동시에 글로벌 투자자들이 한국에 대한 투자를 늘릴 수 있도록 더욱 노력해야 합니다. 한국의 안정적인 경제 환경과 뛰어난 산업 역량은 글로벌 투자자들에게 매력적인 기회를 제공합니다. 한국 정부는 다양한 산업 분야에서 기술 혁신과 지속 가능한 발전을 위해 투자 환경을 더욱 개선해야 나가야 합니다.

셋째, 디지털 금융혁신 시대에 IT 강국 한국은 글로벌 기업들의 비즈니스 유치를 적극적으로 추진해야 합니다. 한국은 이미 세계적인 IT 강국으로 자리잡고 있습니다. IT와 첨단 기술 분야에서 한국은 세계적인 경쟁력을 충분하게 갖추고 있습니다. 이러한 강점을 활용하여 글로벌 기업들의 비즈니스를 더욱 적극적으로 유치해야 합니다. 글로벌 기업들이 한국에 투자하고, 한국을 기반으로 아시아 시장을 공략할 수 있는 기회를 제공해야 합니다. 특히 서울은 혁신적인 스타트업과 첨단기술 기업들이 빠르게

성장할 수 있는 금융허브로 조성되어 있습니다. 이처럼 글로벌 기업들이 한국에서 비즈니스를 확장할 수 있는 정책 환경과 금융 투자 여건이 마련되어 있다는 점을 널리 알려야 합니다.

마이넬리 박사님, 이번 서울 방문을 통해 한국이 국제 사회에서 한층 더 긍정적인 이미지를 확립할 수 있도록 탁월한 혜안을 공유해 주시기 바랍니다. 나아가 런던을 비롯한 세계 각국의 네트워크를 통해 한국에 대한 국제적 신뢰와 평판을 높여 주실 것으로 기대하며, 오늘 행사가 그 중요한 출발점이 되기를 바랍니다.

한국은 IT 강국이자 새로운 글로벌 금융 중심지로 거듭나서 글로벌 투자자들이 주목하는 역동적 금융 국가로서의 역할을 강화해 나갈 것입니다. 이 자리에 함께한 여러분과 함께, 한국이 더욱 강하고 널리 신뢰받는 국가로 자리매김할 수 있기를 희망합니다.

감사합니다.

한국의 국제 신인도 제고와 국가 경쟁력 강화를 위한 전략: 금융의 역할

마이클 마이넬리
(Michael Mainelli)

마이클 마이넬리

Michael Mainelli

　마이클 마이넬리 박사는 영국 런던시의 제694대 시장(Lord Mayor)을 역임하였으며, 현재 런던 상공회의소 회장이자 글로벌 싱크탱크인 Z/Yen 그룹의 회장으로 재직 중이다. 금융, 기술, 지속가능성 분야의 세계적 권위자로, 세계은행, 유엔, 주요 금융 규제기관 등에 자문을 제공해왔다. 하버드대학교에서 수학, 경제학, 물리학을 전공했으며, 이후 런던정경대(LSE)에서 박사학위를 취득하였다.

기조연설

마이클 마이넬리(Michael Mainelli)
前 런던 시장
現 Z/Yen 그룹 회장, 런던 상공회의소 회장

여러분 안녕하십니까. 오늘 이 자리에 함께하게 되어 진심으로 기쁘고 영광스럽게 생각합니다.

먼저, 저의 이번 한국 방문을 아낌 없이 후원해주시고 오늘 행사를 주최해주신 세계경제연구원에 깊은 감사를 드립니다. 전광우 이사장님을 비롯한 모든 임직원 여러분, 진심으로 감사합니다.

Connectivity & Cities
How To Build A Successful Technology & Financial Centre

Professor Michael Mainelli will draw upon decades of Z/Yen research into commercial centres to present a case for policy makers to focus on connectivity when developing their cities. Z/Yen is renowned for its Global Financial Centres, Smart Centres, and Green Finance indices. Z/Yen publishes assessments of over 120 cities, while tracking many more, using over 140 instrumental factors in one of the longest longitudinal research projects on cities and their development. Z/Yen evaluates five areas of competitiveness - business environment, infrastructure, financial sector development, human capital, and reputation.

Professor Mainelli will explore the importance of developing four characteristics - security, rule of law, open trade, and access to skills & talent. He will place these characteristics in the context of cities as tools for connectivity, exploring the inter-connections between commercial success and the urban domain's support for people meeting people.

또한, 오늘 이 행사를 함께 후원해주신 영원그룹에도 깊은 감사를 드립니다. 오늘 제 강연의 제목을 '연결성과 도시

(Connectivity and Cities)'라고 지었는데요, 오늘날과 같은 시대에 사람들을 연결하고 함께 모이게 하는 모든 일은 어려운 일이지만, 그만큼 다양한 긍정적인 결과를 가져온다고 믿습니다. 대내외적으로 어려운 시기에 오늘 이 포럼이 개최될 수 있도록 지원해 주셔서 감사합니다.

오늘 저는 한국이 내부적으로 정치적 위험이 그 어느때보다 높고 대외적으로는 트럼프 2기 행정부 취임 및 여러 전쟁 등 불확실성이 고조된 상황에서 한국의 글로벌 중심지로서의 위상을 공고히 하고 국가 신인도를 제고하기 위한 방안에 대한 강연을 요청받았습니다. 이에 저는 그간 저희 Z/Yen 그룹에서 수행해온 연구 내용을 중심으로 오늘 강연을 진행하고자 합니다. 발표 말미에는 제가 작년에 런던 시장으로서 경험한 일들과 그로부터 얻은 교훈에 대해서도 간략히 말씀드릴 예정입니다.

저는 본질적으로 연구자이며 과학자입니다. 이에 저희 Z/Yen 그룹은 1990년대 후반부터 도시 개발과 관련된 문제를 연구하기 시작했습니다. 당시 저희가 이러한 주제에 관심을 가지게 된 배경은, 영국과 런던이 유로존에 가입하지 않기로 결정했던 상황 때문이었습니다. 그로 인해 런던이 경제적으로 큰 타격을 입을 것이라는 우려가 컸습니다.

Z/Yen Group

"City of London's leading commercial thinktank that spots, solves, and acts"

Zen & Yen– "a philosophical desire to succeed" a ratio recognising that all decisions are tradeoffs
- Services – projects, strategy, expertise on demand, coaching, research, analytics, modern systems
- Sectors – technology, finance, government, voluntary, professional services, outsourcing
- Research– scientific, information technology, markets, financial and commercial centres
- Commercial centre development- Global Financial Centres, Smart Centres, and Global Green Finance indices

이에 따라 2002년, "Sizing Up the City"라는 제목의 보고서를 발간하며 런던이 직면한 주요 경쟁 도시들을 분석했습니다. 당시 언급된 도시는 뉴욕, 파리, 프랑크푸르트 등이었지만, 결과적으로 이 보고서는 매우 부족한 점이 많았습니다. 당시에도 이미 세계 무대에서 중요한 역할을 하던 도쿄, 두바이, 홍콩, 싱가포르 등은 보고서에 언급조차 되지 않았습니다.

이러한 문제 인식을 바탕으로 저희는 세 가지 주요 연구를 시작하게 되었으며, 그중 첫 번째가 국제금융센터지수(Global Financial Centres Index, GFCI)입니다. 참고로, 지난주에는 제37차 보고서를 발표했습니다.

Agenda

- What are commercial centres?
- Why do networks matter?
- Measuring cities:
  o Global Financial Centres Index
  o Smart Centres Index
  o Global Green Finance Index
- How To Build A Successful Technology & Financial Centre

"Get a detailed grip on the big picture."
Chao Kli Ning

    오늘 제가 여러분과 나누고자 하는 주제는 다음과 같습니다. 먼저, '상업 중심지'란 무엇을 의미하는지—이는 금융 중심지를 넘어서는 개념입니다. 둘째, 왜 네트워크와 연결성이 중요한지, 셋째, 이를 어떻게 측정할 수 있는지에 대해 말씀드리겠습니다. 아울러 서울이 현재 어떤 위치에 있는지 짚어보고, 마지막으로 성공적인 중심지를 구축하기 위한 몇 가지 제언으로 발표를 마무리하겠습니다.

    성공적인 중심지의 핵심은 '상호작용'입니다. 도시 연구의 선구자인 경제학자 제인 제이콥스(Jane Jacobs)는 도시란 결국 사람들이 공동으로 만들어가는 공간이라고 강조했습니다. 도시에서 가장 큰 연결 고리는 바로 사람 간의 만남입니다. 그리고 이러한 만남을 촉진하는 모든 요소들은 대체로 긍정적인 효과를 가져옵니다. 항공 교통, 문화 행사, 물류, 해운 산업 등 다양한 측면에서 이러한 연결이 가능합니다. 도시는 사람들이 함께 모이는 장소인 것입니다.

Role Of Commercial Centres

- Commercial centres are places with an intense concentration of trading activity involving interlocking sets of sectors and commercial & financial transactions.
- Bring together three groups:
    - **investors**, who commit funds to activities or products with the expectation of financial returns.
    - **guarantors**, defined as entities insuring or reinsuring projects or companies' operations and risks.
    - **traders** and other risk bearers- those buying, selling, and making markets in securities and those issuing securities, and receiving loans
    ... along with ideas, brainpower, regulators, and miles of advisors consultants, lawyers, accountants, actuaries, scientists, engineers, media, comms, etc.
- Commercial centres need clusters of expertise

이러한 도시들은 보통 세 가지 주요 그룹을 끌어들입니다. 투자자, 무역 종사자, 그리고 제가 '보증자'라고 부르는 전문가 집단—예컨대 회계사, 신용평가사, 변호사 등 시스템이 원활하게 작동하도록 보증하는 이들입니다. 이들 외에도 규제 당국, 컨설턴트, 보험계리사, 과학자, 엔지니어 등 다양한 전문가 집단이 함께합니다. 다시 말해, 상업 중심지란 전문성이 밀집된 클러스터이며, 사람들이 자연스럽게 만나고 싶어 하는 공간이라 할 수 있습니다.

그렇다면, 이러한 중심지의 비전은 무엇일까요? 런던에서는 '상호작용'을 중심에 두고, 하향식이 아닌 '상향식(bottom-up)' 방식으로 도시를 만들어가고자 노력하고 있습니다. 저희가 중요하게 여기는 개념 중 하나는 바로 '세렌디피티(serendipity)'입니다. 이는 우연한 만남이나 인연을 통해 새로운 아이디어와 혁신이 창출되는 현상을 말합니다. 이러한 기회가 자연스럽게 일어날 수 있는 환경을 조성하는 것이야말로, 활기차고 성공적인 도시를 만드는 데 필수적인 요소라고 믿습니다.

일례로 런던 시에서는 '그라운디지(Groundage)'라는 프로그램을 추진하고 있습니다. 이는 도시의 지면 공간을 시민들에게 다시 돌려주고 사람들이 보다 자유롭게 이동할 수 있도록 하기 위한 노력입니다. 이 프로그램은 약 15년 전부터 기획되었으며, 이제 그 성과가 조금씩 가시화되고 있습니다. 런던을 방문해 보신 분들은 아시겠지만, 현재 블룸버그 센터(Bloomberg Center)를 통해 지하를 도보로 통과할 수 있는데요, 불과 8년 전만 해도 이 지역은 보행자 출입이 전면 차단된 상태였습니다. 우리는 이러한 변화를 통해 우연한 만남, 즉 '세렌디피티(serendipity)'를 늘리려고 노력하고 있습니다.

이와 함께 '루파지(Roofage)'라는 프로그램도 추진 중입니다. 이는 도시 전역의 건물 옥상을 시민들에게 개방하려는 노력으로, 현재는 시민들이 자유롭게 이용할 수 있는 옥상 공간이 약 8곳 마련되어 있습니다. 이러한 작은 변화들이 모여 큰 변화를 이끌어내고 있습니다.

A Vision For Commercial Centres

- **Inclusive**, with the business services and regulatory environment fair and open to all-comers, and with support for those wishing to start businesses in the marketplace.
- **Smart**, able to understand and manage increasingly complex technological approaches to finance to open up new markets and offer improved services.
- **Innovative and client/customercentric**, providing a regulatory and legal environment that allows for sustained innovation, balancing regulatory cost and protection – 'Know' not '"No' Your Customer"
- **Digital**, with the majority of services for workers & residents provided via platforms, apps, etc.
- **Green**, with incentives that prioritise the sustainable economy, reduce carbon emissions, and promote green solutions.
- **Centres offering a good quality of life** attracting high-performing people.
- **Resilient & Robust** cities as 'utilities' that must be 'always on'.

상업 중심지에 대한 또 다른 변화는, 이제 도시들이 더 이상 단일 산업에 의존하지 않는다는 점입니다. 과거에는 광산 도시, 전력이나 수도 산업 중심 도시처럼 특정 산업에 기반한 도시들이 많았지만, 오늘날의 도시는 매우 다양한 비전을 공유하고 있습니다. 예컨대, 세계 거의 모든 도시의 시장들에게 동일한 전략 문서를 제시할 수 있을 정도입니다. 포용적이고, 스마트하며, 혁신적이고, 디지털화되어 있고, 친환경적이며, 삶의 질이 높고, 회복탄력성이 뛰어난 도시를 추구한다는 비전입니다. 이러한 공통된 방향성 때문에, 도시간의 차별화는 점점 어려워지고 있기도 합니다.

오늘날 대부분의 도시는 과학기술, 경제 및 금융, 그리고 물류라는 세 가지 공통 분야를 중심으로 발전하고 있습니다. 이는 지난 30년간 중국 본토 도시들의 발전 양상을 보면 더욱 분명히 드러납니다. 다양한 도시들이 매우 유사한 정체성을 띠게 된 것입니다.

제가 작년에 런던 시장을 맡으며 내건 주제는 'Connect to Prosper'였습니다. 사람과 사람, 시스템과 시스템, 지식과 지식을 연결하는 것이 얼마나 중요한지를 강조하고자 했습니다. 런던을 통해 흐르는 수많은 지식 네트워크가 세계 각지로 확산되며, 서울이나 부산과 같은 도시들과의 연결을 가능하게 한다는 점을 기념하고자 했습니다.

Network Theory In A Coffee Cup

이와 관련하여 저는 종종 커피하우스를 비유로 사용했습니다. 한국의 맥락에서는 찻집이 더 적절할 수도 있겠습니다. 1600년대 중반, 커피하우스가 처음 등장했을 당시에는 '페니 대학교(penny university)'라고 불렸습니다. 단돈 1페니로 하루 종일 커피를 마시며 누구와도 자유롭게 대화를 나눌 수 있었고, 그 자리에 있는 모두가 동등하게 취급받았습니다.

참고로 영어 표현 중에 'spend a penny'라는 말이 있는데, 이는 보통 화장실을 간다는 완곡한 표현입니다. 그러나 이 맥락에서는 진짜로 1페니를 내고 지식 교류의 장에 참여하는 것이었습니다.

바로 이러한 커피하우스에서 많은 기관들이 태어났습니다. 주식 거래, 보험거래가 커피하우스에서 시작되었으며, 발틱 커피하우스에서 시작된 발틱 거래소(Baltic Exchange)도 같은 사례입니다.

이처럼 네트워크는 과학자들에게 매우 흥미로운 연구 대상입니다. 네트워크는 삶이 얼마나 복잡하고 역동적인지를 잘 보여줍니다. 우리가 살아가는 세계는 결국 노드(지점) 간 연결로 구성된 구조 위에 세워져 있습니다. 오늘날 많은 관심을 받고 있는 인공지능 역시, 신경망이라는 네트워크 구조에 기반하고 있습니다.

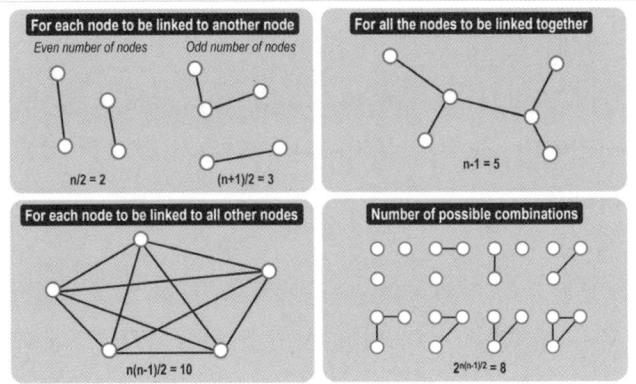

네트워크를 분석해보면, 그 구조는 결코 단순하지 않습니다. 예를 들어 도시의 지도는 수많은 연결로 이루어져 있지만, 그 경계는 명확하지 않습니다. 도시를 정의하는 요소는 무엇일까요? 중세 성벽일까요? 도시계획과 허가 기준일까요? 세금 제도나 노동자와 주민의 위치일까요? 아니면 공기, 물, 바다, 육상 등 다양한 교통 인프라와 폐기물 처리 시스템 등일까요? 사실은 이 모든 것이 해당됩니다.

도시의 인구를 묻는 질문조차 간단하지 않습니다. 런던 시만 보더라도, 면적은 약 2.2 제곱킬로미터에 불과하지만 거주 인구는 약 8,000명, 통근 인구는 68만 7천 명에 이릅니다. 이처럼 극단적으로 업무 중심적인 도시 구조 때문에 코로나19의 타격도 컸습니다.

통근이 중단되면 도시는 큰 타격을 입습니다. 하지만 통근이 원활히 이루어질 경우, 런던 시의 업무 밀도는 맨해튼보다도 높습니다. 맨해튼은 약 6 평방마일에 35만 명이 분산되어 있는 반면, 런던 시는 훨씬 더 집중된 구조입니다. 도쿄는 더 많은 인구를 이동시키지만, 중심 업무지구가 단일하지 않다는 점에서 구조가 다릅니다.

런던 시에 있는 사람들은 모두 업무를 위해 존재합니다. 개 산책이나 우유 한 병을 사러 나온 사람은 없습니다. 그래서 시간은 곧 돈이라는 원칙 아래, 매우 철저한 시간 엄수가 문화로 자리 잡게 되었습니다. 한 예로, 제가 선술집에 서 있으면 25세 청년이 자연스럽게 "무슨 일을 하십니까?"라며 말을 걸어오는 것이 이상할 것이 없는 도시입니다. 모두가 일하러 왔기 때문입니다.

Why Do Networks Matter?

이러한 도시를 이해하기 위해 네트워크 분석은 매우 중요하면서도 동시에 한계를 갖고 있습니다. 과학은 때때로 노드와 링크를 뒤집는 방식으로 네트워크를 모델링할 수 있지만, 그 이상의 직관과 전략적 사고, 예술적 통찰이 필요합니다.

Emergent Properties Of Networks

- Surprise!
- Coordinated, not controlled
- Resilient, and sometimes robust
- Self-referential
- Attention-seeking
- Energy-intensive

"Get a detailed grip on the big picture."
Chao Kli Ning

네트워크 과학에서 자주 언급되는 개념 중 하나가 '창발성(emergent property)'입니다. 이는 본질적으로 '예상치 못한 놀

라움'을 의미합니다. 예를 들어, 뉴런이 시냅스로 연결되어 있다고 해서 그것만으로 의식이 생길 것이라 예상하긴 어렵습니다. 그러나 네트워크는 그렇게 놀라운 결과를 보여줍니다. 질서, 반응성, 성장, 자기 조절, 진화, 항상성 등 다양한 현상이 네트워크에서 출현합니다. 생물학적 복잡성이 진화할 수 있었던 것도 네트워크 덕분이라는 것이 과학자 벨라 수키(Béla Suki)의 주장입니다. 네트워크는 충격에 반응하고, 심지어 충격을 통해 더 강해지기도 합니다.

그렇다면 우리는 이 복잡한 시스템을 어떻게 분석할 수 있을까요? 저희는 우선 연결성(connectivity) 개념에서 출발했습니다. 사람들의 도시 간 상호 평가 데이터를 통해 어떤 도시에서 실제로 비즈니스가 이루어지고 있는지를 분석했습니다. 저희는 1990년대에 런던의 로컬 네트워크를 금융 중심지의 시각을 넘어서 처음으로 분석하기 시작했습니다.

London's Local Network – Knowledge Miles

City of London surrounded by 40 learned societies, 70 higher education institutions, 130 research institutes, and over 24,000 businesses, with more than 300 languages spoken:
- Built on the rule of law
- With an enabling regulatory environment
- Open trade
- Access to incredible talent and skills and unparalleled global connections.

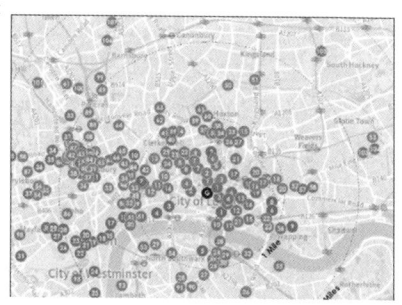

한 예로, 런던 길드홀(Guildhall) 반경 2마일 이내에만 해도 학술기관 40곳(파란색), 대학 70곳(빨간색), 연구기관 130곳이 밀집해 있습니다. 이처럼 극도의 집약도는 자주 간과되곤 합니다. 런던은 금융 중심지이기도 하지만, 런던 시의 산업 구조를 살펴보면, 전체의 약 35~40%는 금융 및 전문 서비스업이 차지하고 있으며, 약 35%는 과학 및 연구 분야가 담당하고 있습니다. 런던이 16세기에서 17세기 사이에 영국 왕립학회(Royal Society of Science)가 자리했던 본거지이기도 했다는 사실은 종종 간과되곤 합니다. 여기에 미디어, 문화, 교육의 중심지로서의 역할도 하고 있습니다.

Factor Assessment Indices

- Combine respondents' perceptions with quantitative data using statistical modelling
- Individual assessments of financial centres are associated with the quantitative data for that centre
- We can then predict how the individual would rate other financial centres based on their profile

GFCI 37
- 130 instrumental factors
- 4,946 respondents
- 31,314 assessments

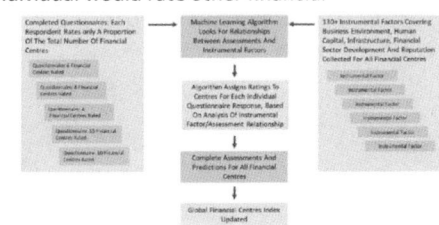

저희는 인식 기반 데이터와 실제 데이터를 결합한 '요인 평가 지수(factor assessment index)'라는 방법론을 개발했습니다. 이는 사람들이 특정 도시에 대해 갖는 인식을 실제 지표와 결합해 그 도시의 경쟁력을 예측하는 방식입니다. 저희는 매 6개월마다 약 5,000명의 전문가를 대상으로 130개 도시를 평가하게 하고, 이 평가 결과를 약 130개의 계량적 지표와 연계해 분석합니다. 이 방식은 응답자가 한 번도 가보지 않은 도시조차 예측 가능한 방식으로 평가할 수 있게 해줍니다.

저도 이 테스트를 직접 해보았습니다. 예를 들어 보험 업계에서 일하고, 조깅을 즐기며, 어린 자녀의 교육을 중요시하는 응답자라면, 해당 응답자의 성향을 반영해 도시를 평가할 수 있습니다. 이는 오늘날의 인공지능과도 유사하지만, 실제로는 '서포트 벡터 머신(Support Vector Machines)'이라는 기계 학습 기법을 활용한 것입니다. 이를 통해 우리는 개인의 성향을 기반으로 도시의 매력을 정량적으로 예측할 수 있게 되었습니다.

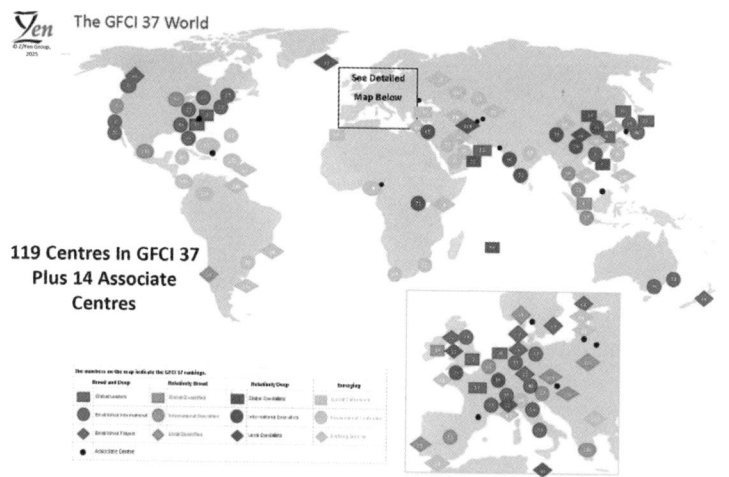

그렇다면, 우리는 어디에 위치하고 있을까요? GFCI 지수에서 본 우리의 위치는 이렇습니다. 2005년, 2006년, 2007년에 처음으로 보고서를 발표했을 때, 우리는 46개의 금융 중심지를 추적했습니다. 오늘날, 앞서 말씀드린 대로 우리는 140개 이상의 금융 중심지를 추적하고 있습니다. 이를 두고 일부에서는 우리가 기준을 낮추었기 때문이라고 생각할 수 있지만, 그렇지 않습니다. 우리가 보고 있는 것은 금융 중심지들의 확산입니다. 이 부분은 잠시 후 다시 언급하겠습니다.

GFCI Top 20

Centre	GFCI 37 Rank	GFCI 37 Rating	GFCI 36 Rank	GFCI 36 Rating	Change in Rank	Change in Rating
New York	1	769	1	763	0	▲6
London	2	762	2	750	0	▲12
Hong Kong	3	760	3	749	0	▲11
Singapore	4	750	4	747	0	▲3
San Francisco	5	749	5	742	0	▲7
Chicago	6	746	6	740	0	▲6
Los Angeles	7	745	7	739	0	▲6
Shanghai	8	744	8	738	0	▲6
Shenzhen	9	743	9	732	0	▲11
Seoul	10	742	11	729	▲1	▲13
Frankfurt	11	741	10	730	▼1	▲11
Dubai	12	740	16	723	▲4	▲17
Washington DC	13	739	12	728	▼1	▲11
Dublin	14	738	14	725	0	▲13
Geneva	15	737	13	726	▼2	▲11
Luxembourg	16	736	19	720	▲3	▲16
Paris	17	735	15	724	▼2	▲11
Amsterdam	18	734	27	712	▲9	▲22
Boston	19	733	22	717	▲3	▲16
Beijing	20	732	18	721	▼2	▲11

아마 여러분은 서울이 어디에 위치하는지 궁금하실 것입니다. 지난주 발표된 결과는 상위 20개 도시를 중심으로 했습니다. 시장님과 다른 분들이 언급하셨듯이, 서울은 매우 잘하고 있습니다. 그런데 서울은 20년 전에는 이 차트에 존재하지 않았습니다. 그래서 그동안 이룬 발전은 정말 대단합니다. 여러분 모두에게 박수를 보내고 싶습니다. 정말 훌륭한 일을 해왔습니다.

하지만 저는 한국에서 서울이 단지 상위 10위에 있는 것에 만족하지 않으실 거라는 점을 잘 알고 있습니다. 여러분은 다른 산업에서처럼 1위, 2위, 아니면 3위 안에 들기를 원하실 것입니다. 그래서 앞서 오세훈 시장님의 축사 말씀에 동의합니다. 서울은 더 발전할 수 있습니다. 그러나 아마도 이를 위해서는 급진적인 변화가 필요할 것입니다. 현재의 방식으로는 할 수 있는 최선을 거의 다 한 상태로 보이기 때문입니다.

부산에 대해서도 언급하고 싶습니다. 부산은 단독으로 분석되는 것은 아니지만 현재 25위에 랭크되어 있습니다. 10년 전에는 51위였다는 점을 고려할 때, 그 발전은 매우 놀랍습니다. 이처럼 의지를 가지고 집중하면 큰 변화를 이끌어낼 수 있을 것입니다.

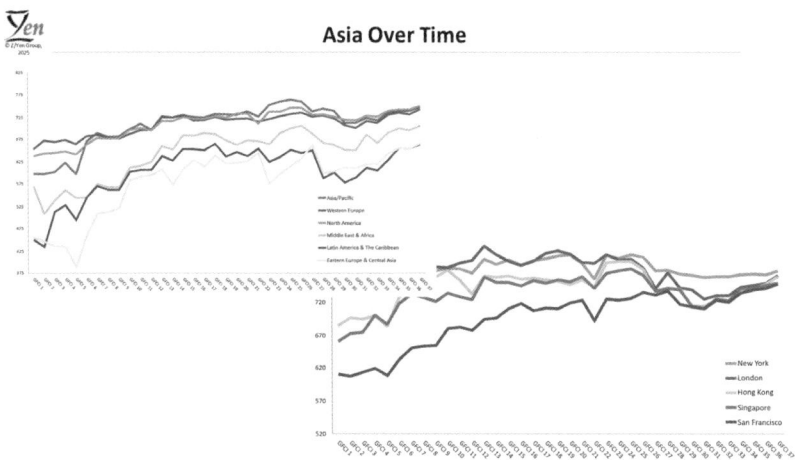

이제 몇 가지 다른 트렌드에 대해 살펴보겠습니다. 장기적인 추세는 무엇일까요? 가장 중요한 장기적인 트렌드 중 하나는 바로 "아시아의 부상"입니다. 처음 GFCI를 출시했을 때 많은 사람들은 서울, 베이징, 상하이가 금융 중심지가 될 수 없다고 했습니다. 불과 20년 전의 이야기입니다. 사실, 10년 전만 해도 이 도시들이 글로벌 금융 중심지로 자리 잡을 것이라고 예측한 사람은 많지 않았습니다.

물론 응답자의 50% 이상이 아시아 출신이기 때문에 아시아에서 너무 많은 응답자가 설문에 참여했다고 비판을 받기도 했지만, 이에 대해 저는 현재 전 세계 금융의 약 60%가 아시아에 위치하고 있다는 점을 상기할 필요가 있다고 강조합니다. GFCI 설문 응답자의 다양성을 더 확보해야 할 필요는 있다는 점은 인정하며 이는 저희가 노력할 부분입니다.

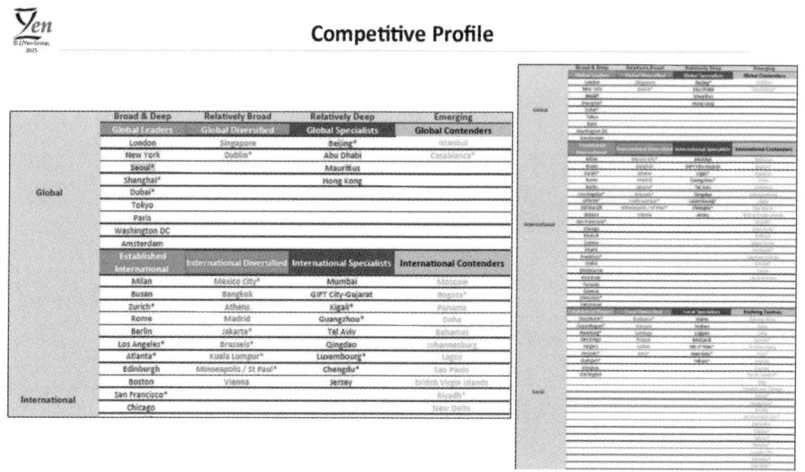

그런데, 하나의 숫자만으로는 결코 판단해서는 안 됩니다. 순위표에서 아래쪽에 있을수록, 그 도시가 가진 깊이와 다양성을 평가하는 것이 더 중요합니다. 우리는 각 도시의 경쟁력 프로필을 기반으로 순위를 매기는 방법을 사용합니다. 여기서 보시다시피, 우리는 국제적, 지역적, 글로벌 관점에서 12개 이상의 다양한 카테고리로 평가합니다. 서울은 이 모든 순위에서 매우 좋은 성과를 보이고 있습니다. 처음에는 서울이 주로 지역 중심지로 평가되었지만, 서울은 꾸준히 성장해 왔습니다.

Sectors

Rank	Banking	Investment Management	Insurance	Professional Services	Government & Regulatory	Finance	FinTech	Trading
1	London	Hong Kong	Hong Kong	Singapore	New York	Hong Kong	New York	New York
2	New York	New York	New York	New York	London	Shenzhen	London	Singapore
3	Hong Kong	London	London	London	Singapore	Singapore	Singapore	London
4	Shanghai	Shenzhen	Singapore	Seoul	Zurich	New York	Frankfurt	Shanghai
5	Los Angeles	Singapore	Shenzhen	San Francisco	Shanghai	Shanghai	Dubai	Seoul
6	Singapore	Dublin	Beijing	Dubai	Los Angeles	Frankfurt	Shanghai	Hong Kong
7	Washington DC	Shanghai	San Francisco	Hong Kong	Frankfurt	Washington DC	Hong Kong	Los Angeles
8	Shenzhen	Dubai	Chicago	Los Angeles	San Francisco	Seoul	Dublin	Chicago
9	Chicago	Chicago	Tokyo	Chicago	Hong Kong	Beijing	Amsterdam	Paris
10	Frankfurt	San Francisco	Los Angeles	Luxembourg	Chicago	Tokyo	San Francisco	Geneva
11	Beijing	Frankfurt	Shanghai	Shenzhen	Geneva	San Francisco	Paris	San Francisco
12	Paris	Los Angeles	Frankfurt	Zurich	Seoul	Singapore	Los Angeles	Shenzhen
13	San Francisco	Paris	Boston	Geneva	Washington DC	Chicago	Washington DC	Dubai
14	Tokyo	Seoul	Zurich	Shenzhen	Dubai	Chicago	Luxembourg
15	Geneva	Luxembourg	Geneva	Paris	Amsterdam	Los Angeles	Tokyo	Washington DC

비유하자면, 축구팀의 승률을 평가하기 위해서 각 선수가 어떤 역할을 하고 있는지, 팀이 어떻게 협력하고 있는지, 전략이 효과적인지 등을 파악해야 하는 것과 같습니다. 성공은 여러 분야에서 뛰어난 성과를 거두는 것에 기반하기 때문입니다. 즉, 다양한 산업 부문별로 선도적인 도시들이 어떻게 평가되는지를 확인해야합니다. 서울은 이 많은 분야에서 우수한 성과를 거두고 있기 때문에 10위에 랭크될 수 있었습니다. 이는 점점 더 중요해질 것입니다. 도시가 성공하려면, 여러 가지 분야에서 동시에 뛰어난 성과를 거두어야 하며, 이러한 성과들은 서로를 강화합니다. 성공은 여러 분야에서의 뛰어난 성과가 쌓여 이루어지는 것입니다.

FinTech Ranking and Rating

Centre	GFCI 37 FinTech Rank	GFCI 37 FinTech Rating	GFCI 36 FinTech Rank	GFCI 36 FinTech Rating	Change in Rank	Change in Rating
New York	1	749	1	737	0	▲12
London	2	748	2	725	0	▲23
Shenzhen	3	747	3	722	0	▲25
Hong Kong	4	746	9	716	▲5	▲30
San Francisco	5	729	4	721	▼1	▲8
Los Angeles	6	727	6	719	0	▲8
Washington DC	7	726	5	720	▼2	▲6
Singapore	8	724	8	717	0	▲7
Chicago	9	723	7	718	▼2	▲5
Seoul	10	716	10	707	0	▲9
Guangzhou	11	713	14	701	▲3	▲12
Boston	12	712	12	705	0	▲7
Zurich	13	710	13	704	0	▲6
Dubai	14	709	21	692	▲7	▲17
Beijing	15	708	11	706	▼4	▲2
Shanghai	16	707	15	699	▼1	▲8
Toronto	17	706	18	695	▲1	▲11
Chengdu	18	705	17	696	▼1	▲9
Paris	19	704	22	691	▲3	▲13
Montreal	20	703	19	694	▼1	▲9

두 번째로 우리가 주목하고 있는 분야는 핀테크입니다. 서울은 이 분야에서 매우 좋은 성과를 내고 있으며, 저는 이것이 한국의 경쟁 우위의 핵심이 될 수 있다고 믿습니다. 서울과 부산을 포함한 한국 전역에서 보유한 IT 기술이 큰 장점이 될 것입니다.

그러나 제가 강조하고 싶은 점은, 특히 제가 1980년대 초반 금융에 컴퓨터를 도입하며 금융 분야에 처음 발을 들인 기술자로서, 핀테크는 새로운 개념이 아니라는 것입니다. 사실, 이는 제가 평생 해온 일이기도 합니다. 바로 금융을 디지털화하는 것이죠.

우리가 지금까지 이룬 성과는 금융 분야가 매우 고도로 디지털화되었다는 점이며, 이는 은행과 보험사의 구조에 큰 영향을 미쳤습니다. 이들 기관은 점차 자동화되고 있지만, 아직도 금융과 실물 경제의 통합에는 한계가 있습니다.

여러분도 기억하시겠지만, 17년 전 금융위기 당시에는 금융이 실물 경제를 제대로 지원하지 못한다고 불평이 있었습니다. 그런데 지금도 해운업이나 항공업을 살펴보면 이들 산업은 뛰어난 시스템을 보유하고 있음에도 불구하고 금융에 접목하려 할 때마다, 예를 들어 송장 발행이나 지급 과정에서 큰 어려움을 겪고 있습니다. 이러한 과정은 여전히 매끄럽지 않습니다.

제가 바라는 것은 금융이 더욱더 종합적이고 통합된 방식으로 발전하여 API 기반의 서비스 모델로 변화하는 것입니다. 사람들이 필요할 때 금융 서비스를 구매하고, 그동안 40년 이상 논의되어온 마이크로파이낸스, 즉 매우 작은 금액의 결제도 성공적으로 처리할 수 있는 시스템이 구현되는 것입니다. 신용장이나 신용한도와 같은 서비스도 포함됩니다. 실물 경제와 금융이 더욱 잘 통합되려면 아직 갈 길이 멉니다.

런던에서 저희 Z/Yen 그룹이가 하고 있는 일을 예를 들어보겠습니다. 우리는 2년 전에 스마트 경제 네트워크 프로그램을 시작하여, 전 세계 사람들과 기업들의 디지털 인증 시스템을 구축하고 있습니다. 이를 Nordic XROAD 시스템과 결합하여, 정부들이 사용하고 있는 시스템을 무역에 적용하고 있습니다. 우리는 이에 관한 네 가지 보고서를 발표했으며, 최근에는 디지털 인증에 관한 보고서도 발표했습니다.

Competitiveness Factor Groups

Rank	Business Environment	Human Capital	Infrastructure	Financial Sector Development	Reputational & General
1	New York	New York	New York	New York	New York
2	London	Hong Kong	Hong Kong	Hong Kong	London
3	Hong Kong	London	London	London	Hong Kong
4	Singapore	Singapore	Singapore	Shanghai	Singapore
5	San Francisco	San Francisco	Shenzhen	Singapore	San Francisco
6	Chicago	Chicago	Seoul	Chicago	Dublin
7	Los Angeles	Los Angeles	Paris	San Francisco	Chicago
8	Frankfurt	Washington DC	Shanghai	Los Angeles	Frankfurt
9	Amsterdam	Boston	Dubai	Shenzhen	Paris
10	Dubai	Zurich	Los Angeles	Washington DC	Seoul
11	Shenzhen	Shenzhen	Geneva	Seoul	Dubai
12	Boston	Dubai	San Francisco	Frankfurt	Geneva
13	Shanghai	Frankfurt	Beijing	Zurich	Los Angeles
14	Washington DC	Shanghai	Zurich	Beijing	Shanghai
15	Paris	Seoul	Frankfurt	Geneva	Washington DC

우리는 또한 다양한 지역에서 경쟁력을 분석하고 있습니다. 서울은 이 분야에서도 매우 좋은 성과를 내고 있으며, 특히 규제 시스템의 강점이 돋보입니다. 서울의 규제 시스템은 전 세계적으로 매우 좋은 것으로 평가되고 있으며, 이는 향후 더 많은 발전을 위한 희망을 제공합니다.

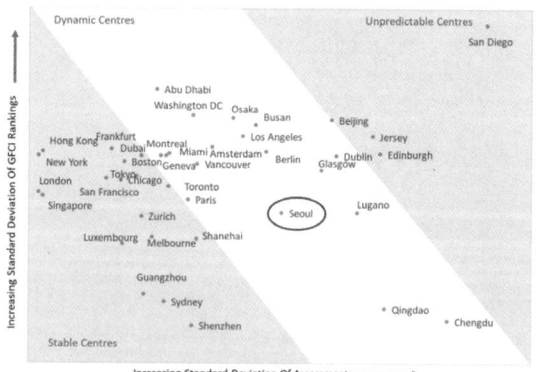

이제 서울이 안정적이냐 아니면 역동적이냐에 대해 간략히 말씀드리겠습니다. 우리는 각 도시를 평가할 때, 그 도시가 가진 요인의 변동성과 그 요인이 미치는 영향을 고려합니다. 어떤 도시가 불안정하다면, 이는 상단 오른쪽에 위치하게 되며, 피해야 할 대상입니다. 그러나 상단 왼쪽의 안정성 또한 바람직하지 않습니다. 이는 기동성이 부족하다는 의미이기 때문입니다.

저는 서울이 매우 이상적인 위치에 있다고 생각합니다. 서울은 요인들을 변화시키고 실질적인 변화를 이끌어낼 수 있는 기회를 가지고 있으며, 침체되지 않았습니다.

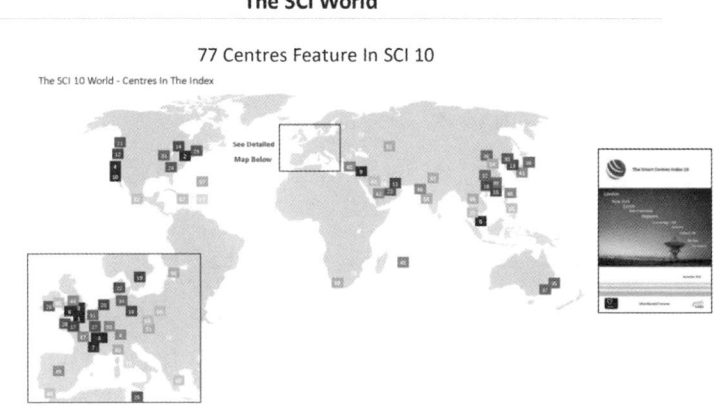

Asia/Pacific – Top 15

Centre	SCI 10 Rank	SCI 10 Rating	SCI 9 Rank	SCI 9 Rating	Change in Rank	Change in Rating
Singapore	5	695	7	698	▲2	▼3
Busan	13	686	14	691	▲1	▼5
Hong Kong	15	684	12	693	▼3	▼9
Shenzhen	18	679	22	683	▲4	▼4
Seoul	30	667	29	676	▼1	▼9
Guangzhou	32	665	37	668	▲5	▼3
Sydney	35	662	36	669	▲1	▼7
Beijing	36	661	30	675	▼6	▼14
Melbourne	37	660	43	662	▲6	▼2
Tokyo	38	659	33	672	▼5	▼13
Shanghai	39	658	35	670	▼4	▼12
Osaka	41	656	50	655	▲9	▲1
Taipei	45	652	47	658	▲2	▼6
GIFT City-Gujarat	46	650	42	663	▼4	▼13
New Delhi	53	643	62	643	▲9	0

- Singapore, Busan, Hong Kong, and Shenzhen rank in the top 20 in the world
- Thirteen centres in the region maintained their position or rose in the rankings in SCI 10, with only Osaka improving in the ratings

　또한, 금융만이 전부가 아니라는 점을 강조하고 싶습니다. 우리는 스마트 센터 인덱스를 운영하고 있으며, 이 인덱스는 약 77개의 센터를 평가합니다. 아시아 지역에서 상위 15개 도시를 살펴보면, 서울은 매우 잘 위치해 있습니다.

　다만, 환경 관련 지표 분석 결과, 한국은 이 부문에서는 개선할 여지가 있다고 생각합니다. 특히 탄소 거래와 전반적인 배출 감소에 관한 실질적인 대응이 필요합니다. 이는 어려운 문제입니다. 한국은 중공업이 많은 나라로, 이러한 변화를 이끌어내는 것이 쉽지 않을 것입니다. 물론 몇 가지 진전이 있었지만, 이 분야에서 더 많은 노력이 필요해 보입니다.

The GGFI World
97 Centres Feature In GGFI 14

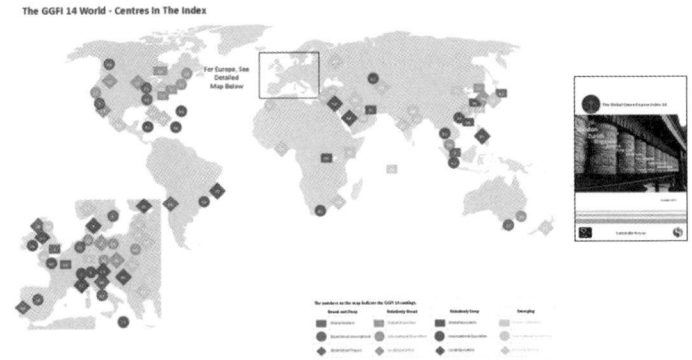

Headlines – Asia/Pacific Top 20

Centre	GGFI 14 Rank	GGFI 14 Rating	GGFI 13 Rank	GGFI 13 Rating	Change In Rank	Change In Rating
Singapore	3	630	5	641	▲2	▼11
Seoul	21	610	22	621	▲1	▼11
Shenzhen	24	607	25	618	▲1	▼11
Sydney	29	602	23	620	▼6	▼18
Busan	30	600	30	613	0	▼13
Beijing	33	597	31	612	▼2	▼15
Shanghai	34	596	28	615	▼6	▼19
Melbourne	37	593	32	611	▼5	▼18
Hong Kong	38	592	37	606	▼1	▼14
Qingdao	40	590	39	604	▼1	▼14
Tokyo	42	588	41	602	▼1	▼14
Osaka	51	579	46	597	▼5	▼18
Guangzhou	54	576	50	593	▼4	▼17
Wellington	55	575	35	608	▼20	▼33
Jakarta	63	567	65	577	▲2	▼10
GIFT City-Gujarat	65	565	66	576	▲1	▼11
New Delhi	68	562	75	567	▲7	▼5
Kuala Lumpur	78	552	63	580	▼15	▼28
Manila	81	549	69	573	▼12	▼24
Bangkok	82	548	72	570	▼10	▼22

환경평가지표인 GGFI(Global Green Finance Index)에서는 97개 센터의 환경 성과를 평가합니다. 아시아 태평양 지역에 국한하자면 서울이 상대적으로 잘 하고 있다고 평가되지만, 전 세계 도시로 범위를 넓히면 서울은 이 부분에서 더 나은 성과가 요구됩니다. 녹색 금융에 대한 세계적인 관심이 커지고 있으며,

이는 금융과 과학 분야에서 성공을 거두려는 추세와 맞물려 있습니다.

친환경적이고 책임감 있는 도시가 인기를 끌고 있는 것은 놀라운 일이 아닙니다. 예를 들어, 칠레, 우루과이, 태국은 정부의 탄소 목표를 달성하지 못할 경우 이자율이 상승하는 지속 가능성 연계 채권을 발행했습니다. 이는 정부 정책이 하루아침에 바뀌지 않도록 하고, 재생 가능 에너지와 같은 분야에서 25년 장기 투자 약속을 필요로 하는 투자자들에게 유리한 접근법입니다.

Green Finance In Leading Centres

Centre	Green Finance Index	Green Finance Depth	Green Finance Quality	Financial Centre Competitiveness
New York	5	8	5	1
London	1	3	1	2
Hong Kong	38	39	39	3
Singapore	3	3	3	4
San Francisco	17	16	18	5
Chicago	15	17	13	6
Los Angeles	7	5	10	7
Shanghai	34	35	33	8
Shenzhen	24	11	36	9
Frankfurt	20	14	24	10
Seoul	21	21	20	11
Washington DC	12	14	11	12
Geneva	4	5	4	13
Dublin	56	54	59	14
Paris	18	21	14	15
Dubai	35	44	22	16
Zurich	2	2	2	17
Beijing	33	28	39	18
Luxembourg	8	9	6	19
Tokyo	42	54	26	20
Source	GGFI 14 Rank	GGFI 14 Depth Rank	GGFI 14 Quality Rank	GFCI 36 Rank

Reputational Advantage/Disadvantage

- Global Financial Centres Index: +10 (balanced)
- Smart Centres Index: -165 (more marketing)
- Global Green Finance Index: +49 (more action)

 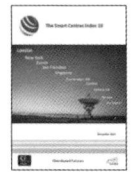 

서울은 글로벌 금융중심지들 중 꽤 좋은 성과를 내고 있지만 환경 문제에 대해서는 더 많은 실질적인 조치가 필요합니다. 스마트 센터 인덱스에서도 서울이 평판 지수에서 상대적으로 낮은 점수를 기록하고 있습니다. 서울은 IT와 금융이 결합된 센터로서 더 많은 마케팅이 필요합니다. 서울의 강점을 알리기 위한 마케팅이 더 많이 이루어져야 할 시점입니다.

마지막으로, 규제에 대해 말씀드리겠습니다. 규제는 금융 센터 구축에서 중요한 역할을 하지만, 그것은 U자형 곡선처럼 작용합니다. 규제가 너무 많을 수도 있고, 너무 적을 수도 있습니다. 규제를 잘 조절하는 것이 중요한 이유입니다.

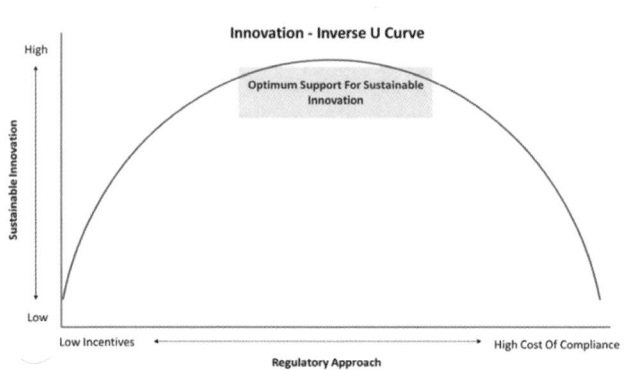

우리는 디지털 자산 분야에서 이미 이러한 갈등을 목격해 왔습니다. 앞으로는 AI에서도 유사한 상황이 발생할 것입니다. AI 규제가 곧 도입될 것이며, 지난 2년 동안 런던에서 전 세계 금융 서비스 산업에 ISO 42001을 AI 규제 접근법으로 채택하자고 권고하는 프로그램을 진행했습니다.

만약 국제 결제에서 ISO 20022를, 리스크와 보안을 다룬 ISO 27000과 65000을 통해 얻은 것처럼 하나의 인증 패스포트를 도입할 수 있다면, 경쟁하는 다양한 규제들 대신 하나의 인증 패스포트를 사용할 수 있을 것입니다. 이는 서비스 수출 시 발생할 수 있는 규제 장벽을 피하는 방법이 될 것입니다.

현재 미국의 절반 이상 주(州)에서는 보험에 대해 AI 규제를 준수해야 하며, EU와의 연계도 요구됩니다. 그런데 이번 방문에서 저는 한국의 AI 규제 접근법이 다소 유연하다는 점을 알게 되어 기뻤습니다. 저는 이것이 적절한 접근이라고 생각하며, ISO를 통한 시장 기반 솔루션이 AI 규제에 의한 무역 장벽을 해결하는 데 도움을 줄 것이라고 믿습니다.

 Emerging (Mutual) Opportunities

- Asset management, pensions
- Policy performance bonds– sovereign sustainabilitylinked bonds, sovereign policyperformance bonds
- Carbon emissions trading schemes & sequestration/voluntary carbon markets trading & insurance
- Hydrogen trading
- Digital and crypto assets
- Public-private partnership catastrophe reinsurance
- Ethical AI
- Art markets

"Get a big picture grip on the details."
Chao Kli Ning

마치기 전에 제가 런던시장으로서 얻은 경험과 관련한 몇 가지를 말씀드리겠습니다. 네 가지 교훈, 일곱 가지 비전, 그리고 하나의 기본적인 전략입니다.

 Fourteen Centuries Of Strategy Lessons For A Mayor

- Defence
- Rule of Law
- Open trade
- Access to skills & talent

먼저, 네 가지 교훈을 말씀드리겠습니다. 세계에서 가장 오래된 민주적인 노동자 및 주민 협동조합의 수장이 되어보니, 매우 다른 삶의 관점을 가지게 되었습니다. 런던시는 640년 경부터 노동자들에게 투표권을 부여해왔으니, 거의 1,400년의 역사를 자랑합니다. 이를 통해 우리는 매우 장기적인 관점을 가지게 되며, 오랜 세월 동안 배운 교훈들이 있습니다.

첫 번째 교훈은 '방어'입니다. 서구에서는 종종 이를 간과하는 경향이 있지만, 최근 러-우 전쟁으로 인해 그 중요성이 다시 부각되었습니다. 자본 통제와 같은 문제는 매우 현실적이고 중요한 사안입니다. 전쟁 지역에 누구도 자금을 가져가지 않는다는 사실은 아주 기본적인 진리입니다.

두번째는, '법치주의(rule of law)입니다. 법치주의는 매우 광범위한 개념으로, 단순히 소송에 관한 것이 아닙니다. 이는 단순히 소송 절차에 국한된 개념이 아니라 훨씬 더 포괄적인 것입니다. 물론 공정한 재판과 법 앞의 평등한 대우도 포함되지만, 그것만으로는 충분하지 않습니다. 이 개념은 한 사회 전체의 문화를 아우릅니다.

그 장소는 신뢰를 형성할 수 있는 환경인가? 사람들이 책임을 다할 것이라는 믿음을 가질 수 있는가? 라는 질문을 끊임없이 던져야합니다. 왜냐하면, 이상적으로는 누구도 법정까지 가는 일을 원하지 않기 때문입니다. 법원은 어디까지나 최후의 수단이어야 합니다. 진정 중요한 것은 대체적 분쟁 해결 메커니즘의 존재입니다―중재, 조정, 화해, 전문가 판정 등은 금융 서비스 분야에서는 익숙한 방식들이지만, 우리는 종종 이 모든 것의 핵심이 법의 지배임을 잊곤 합니다.

한국이 지금 여러 도전에 직면해 있다는 점을 잘 알고 있습니다. 영국도 유사한 시기를 겪었습니다. 보리스 존슨(Boris Johnson) 총리 재임 시기에는 의회 정회 사태가 있었고, 사법부가 공격과 모욕을 받는 일도 있었습니다. 또한, 지금 미국에서 벌어지고 있는 상황도 우리 모두가 지켜보고 있습니다. 그러나 여러분 모두가 잘 아시다시피, 이러한 도전에 제대로 대응하지 않는 것은 큰 위험을 수반합니다. 법치주의는 우리가 하는 모든 일의 토대이기 때문입니다.

세 번째 교훈은 '자유무역의 중요성'입니다. 장기적인 경제적 성공을 위해서는 개방된 무역을 지지하고 촉진하는 것이 필수적입니다. 네 번째 교훈은 '역량있는 인재에 대한 접근성'입니다. 경쟁력 있는 인재를 유치하고 육성할 수 있는 환경이 뒷받침되어야 지속 가능한 성장이 가능합니다.

A Vision For Commercial Centres

- **Inclusive**, with the business services and regulatory environment fair and open to all-comers, and with support for those wishing to start businesses in the marketplace.
- **Smart**, able to understand and manage increasingly complex technological approaches to finance to open up new markets and offer improved services.
- **Innovative and client/customercentric**, providing a regulatory and legal environment that allows for sustained innovation, balancing regulatory cost and protection – 'Know' not '"No' Your Customer"
- **Digital**, with the majority of services for workers & residents provided via platforms, apps, etc.
- **Green**, with incentives that prioritise the sustainable economy, reduce carbon emissions, and promote green solutions.
- **Centres offering a good quality of life** attracting high-performing people.
- **Resilient & Robust** cities as 'utilities' that must be 'always on'.

앞서 일곱 가지 비전에 대해서는 앞서 이미 소개한 바 있습니다. 그 내용은 지금까지 말씀드린 것에 잘 적용되며, 여러분이 실제로 따를 수 있는 실천 가능한 요소들입니다. 하지만 여기서 제가 가장 강조하고 싶은 것은, 절대 그 연결성 다이어그램을 잊지 말아야 한다는 것입니다.

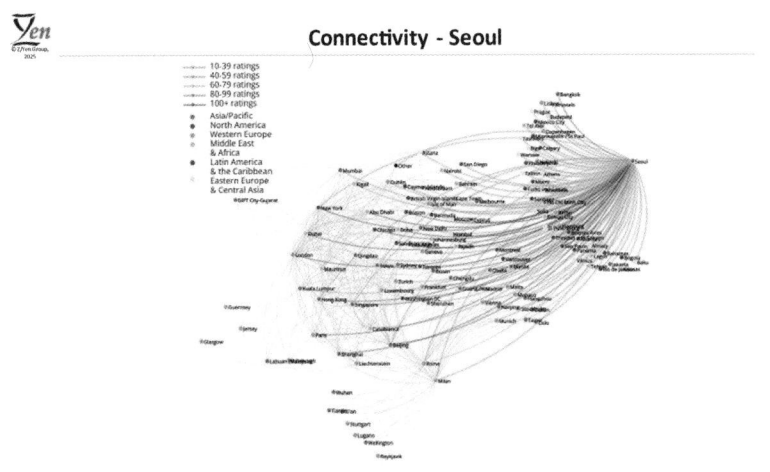

이 다이어그램을 통해 100년 동안의 핵심적인 변화를 볼 수 있습니다. 서울이 얼마나 잘 하고 있는지 확인할 수 있습니다. 하지만 성공하려면 10위, 9위, 8위가 아니라, 자신만의 연결성을 측정하는 것이 중요합니다. GFCI와 Smart Centers Index에서의 결과들이 그것을 입증할 것입니다.

Commercial Centre Connectivity

- You have to be connected
- You can't be an international centre without international people
- Successful people want to live in successful, cosmopolitan cities
- Reputation is vital – and you can lose a good one overnight

"Get a detailed grip on the big picture."
Chao Kli Ning

　마지막으로 가장 중요한 '전략'을 말씀드리겠습니다. 그것은 바로 '연결성'입니다. 글로벌 허브 도시가 되기 위해서는 다른 국제적인 상업 중심지들과 연결되어야 합니다. 그리고 이를 위해서는 국제적인 인재들이 필요합니다. 서울은 이 부분에서는 잘 발전해왔다고 봅니다.

　성공한 사람들은 성공적인 국제도시(cosmopolitan cities)에서 살기를 원합니다. 이와 관련해 K-컬처가 전 세계에 미친 영향력을 결코 과소평가해서는 안 됩니다. K-팝, K-드라마를 통해, 과거에는 한국이라는 나라를 전혀 알지 못했던 사람들이 이제는 넷플릭스를 통해 일상 속에서 한국을 접하고, 한국 문화를 자연스럽게 흡수하고 있습니다. 특히 한국의 법정을 다룬 드라마들은 법치주의에 대한 한국의 존중을 서구인들이 이해할 수 있는 방식으로 보여주는 좋은 사례이기도 합니다. 이처럼 많은 긍정적인 변화가 일어나고 있으며, 이 모든 것이 국가의 평판

(reputation)에 결정적인 역할을 합니다. 좋은 평판은 한순간에 잃을 수도 있는 자산이기에, 더욱 신중히 지켜나가야 할 것입니다.

"Treat All Comers Fairly"

그렇다면 성공을 위한 전략은 하나의 근본적인 전략은 무엇일까요? 매우 간단합니다. '모든 상거래를 공정하게 대하는 것'입니다. 금융 중심지를 개방하고 동시에 탄탄한 방어 체계를 갖추고, 모든 이가 공정하게 대우받을 수 있도록 보장하면 됩니다. 이러한 요소들이 충족될 때, 진정한 의미에서의 성공적인 금융 중심지가 만들어질 수 있습니다. 물론 여기에 섬세한 접근이 필요합니다. 단순히 규제당국에 "공정하게 하라"고 지시하는 것만으로는 충분하지 않습니다. 그 이상을 고민해야 합니다.

예를 들어보겠습니다. 경쟁 규제(competition regulation)처럼 단순해 보이는 분야조차도 현실은 결코 단순하지 않습니다. 영국의 사례를 들자면, 영국은 세계적으로 가장 훌륭한 도매금융

역량을 보유하고 있다고 평가받는 반면, 소매금융 분야는 매우 취약한 편입니다. 실제로 세계 최악 수준의 소매금융 시스템 중 하나라는 지적도 있습니다. 현재 영국의 소매금융 산업은 단 3개의 은행이 전체 시장의 70% 이상을, 4개의 은행이 82%를 점유하고 있습니다. 이것이 과연 경쟁적인 시장이라고 할 수 있을까요? 외국계 은행 입장에서 이와 같은 시장에 진입하고 싶을까요? 전혀 그렇지 않습니다. 문제 발생 시, 결과는 불 보듯 뻔하기 때문입니다.

따라서 우리가 바라는 것은 '다양한 참여자들이 존재하는 경쟁적인 시장 구조'입니다. 예컨대, 하나의 거대 연기금이 시장을 지배하는 환경은 바람직하지 않습니다. 외국 기업이 해당 시장에 진입해 문제가 생기면, 결과는 명확합니다. 그들이 승자가 아닐 가능성이 높으며, 그런 환경에서는 자연히 시장 진입을 꺼리게 됩니다.

런던시만 보더라도, 단 1제곱마일의 구역에 약 2만 4천 개의 기업이 밀집해 있습니다. 전 세계 외환거래의 40%, 해상보험 및 재보험 시장의 95%가 이곳을 거쳐 갑니다. 이 모든 수치를 제가 언급할 수 있는 이유는, 제가 런던 시장으로서 홍보해 왔기 때문입니다. 그러나 흥미로운 사실은, 이 2만 4천 개의 기업 중 2만 3,750개가 중소기업(SMEs)이라는 점입니다. 직원 수 500명 이상인 대기업은 단 250곳에 불과합니다.

이처럼 수많은 중소기업들이 거대한 도매금융 시장을 실질적으로 움직이고 있으며, 우리가 흔히 접하는 모건스탠리, 골드만

삭스, JP모건 등의 간판 뒤에 있는 실제 동력은 바로 이들 중소기업입니다. 브렉시트(Brexit) 이후에도 이 부문은 성장을 이어가고 있습니다. 2016년 당시 52만 5천 명이었던 관련 종사자 수는 최근 조사(2023년 11월 기준)에서 68만 7천 명으로 증가했습니다. 그들은 투표권을 가졌기 때문에 정확한 집계가 가능했습니다. 그리고 이 중 누군가 의심할지 모르겠지만, 그들이 모두 컴플라이언스 업무만을 하는 것도 아닙니다.

또한 지난 8년간 런던시의 글로벌 자산 운용 규모는 11%에서 13%로 증가했습니다. 이 모든 성과는 "런던에서는 공정하게 대우받을 수 있다"는 신뢰를 바탕으로 이뤄진 것입니다.

저는 개인적으로 브렉시트를 지지하지 않았고, 지금도 그 입장은 변하지 않았습니다. 그럼에도 불구하고, 영국이 유럽연합을 떠난 이후, 일부 기업들은 프랑크푸르트나 파리에서는 동등하게 대우받지 못할 것이라는 우려로 인해 오히려 런던을 유럽 본부의 기반으로 선택하고 있는 실정입니다.

즉, 성공을 위한 기본 전략은 간단합니다. 모든 상거래를 공정하게 대해서, 다양한 기업들이 존재하는 시장을 만들어가야 합니다. 거대한 기업 하나만 존재하는 시장이 아니라, 상호작용하는 다양한 기업들이 있는 시장을 만들면 성공적인 글로벌 상업, 금융 중심지가 될 수 있습니다.

그럼 이상으로 강연을 마치겠습니다. 오늘 이른 시간부터 자리해 주신 여러분께 진심으로 감사드리며, 특히 세계경제연구원과 영원무역그룹에 감사말씀을 올립니다.

Q&A

전광우 이사장: 매우 유익한 발표를 해주신 마이넬리 교수님께 감사드립니다. 이제 질의응답 시간을 갖겠습니다. 주미대사 및 유럽연합 대사를 지내신 안호영 대사님께서 질문하시겠습니다.

안호영 대사: 마이넬리 시장님, 이렇게 뵙게 되어 매우 기쁩니다. 강연 마지막 슬라이드에서 "모든 상거래를 평등하게 대우해야 한다"고 하셨는데요, 이 개념은 국제무역에서의 '최혜국 대우(Most Favored Nation, MFN)' 원칙과 유사하다는 인상을 받았습니다. 그런데 현재 미국에서 트럼프 대통령이 추진 중인 정책을 보면, 그는 사실상 MFN 원칙을 해체하고 있는 것처럼 보입니다. 저는 이 현상이 단순히 무역의 영역을 넘어서, 더 넓은 의미에서 법치주의에 대한 공격이 아닐까 하는 의문이 들었습니다. 이에 대해 어떻게 보시는지요?

마이클 마이넬리 박사: 먼저, 대사님 질문 감사드립니다. 제가 배경 설명을 드리자면, 저는 런던의 전통적인 길드 중 하나인 World Traders 길드의 마스터(수장)를 역임한 바 있습니다. 저희는 국제 무역에 대해 꽤 많은 연구를 진행해왔고, 특히 무역 흐름과 관세 문제에 대해 집중해왔습니다. 관세는 매우 흥미로운 주제이기도 합니다.

1973년, 영국이 유럽연합(EU)에 가입했을 당시를 돌이켜보면, 호주나 뉴질랜드 사람들에게는 마치 우리가 그들을 배신한 것처럼 느껴졌을 것입니다. 그들은 당시 영국에 양고기를 수출하고 있었지만, 우리가 "이제 EU 회원국이니 당신들의 양고기를 더 이상 받을 수 없다"고 통보했었기 때문입니다. 그야말로 냉정하게 문을 닫아버린 셈이었습니다.

당시 호주 고등판무관(대사급)을 만난 적이 있는데, 흥미롭게도 그의 아들이 브렉시트 시기에 역시 고등판무관을 맡고 있었습니다. 그 아들이 저에게 이런 말을 했습니다. "우리는 그때부터 정신을 차리고 스스로 길을 찾기 시작했어요."

그래서 제가 "무슨 뜻입니까?"라고 묻자, 그는 이렇게 답했습니다. "우리는 전 세계를 찾아다니며 말했습니다. '여러분이 보조금을 받고 만들어낸 값싼 제품들, 저희는 기꺼이 받겠습니다. 보내주세요. 저희 제품도 혹시 필요하시면 언제든 말씀해 주세요.' 그리고 실제로 호주는 세계에서 가장 많은 자유무역협정을 체결한 국가가 되었습니다."

호주는 불과 350명도 되지 않는 작은 무역부서로 이런 일을 해냈습니다. 정말로 자유무역을 진지하게 받아들였기 때문입니다. 물론, 그들도 완벽하지는 않습니다. 어느 누구도 완벽하진 않지요. 하지만 저는 서방 국가들이 지금 직면한 도전 가운데 하나가 바로 이 점이라고 생각합니다.

만약 트럼프 대통령의 관세 정책이 잘못되었다고 우리가 믿는다면, 지적으로도 그렇고 공정성 면에서도 그렇다면, 우리는 이것을 하나의 거대한 글로벌 실험이라고 볼 수도 있지 않을까요?

그렇다면 오히려 우리 쪽이 더 적극적으로, 더 의지를 갖고 자유 무역으로 나아가야 하지 않겠습니까?

예컨대 CPTPP(포괄적·점진적 환태평양경제동반자협정) 같은 다자협정에 우리가 어떻게 대응할지도 중요합니다. 우리가 모두 자유무역을 지향하며 과감하게 규제를 풀고 개방성을 높인다면, 그것이 트럼프 대통령의 정책이 잘못되었음을 가장 분명히 보여주는 길이 될 것입니다.

특히 서울 같은 도시에서 서비스 분야—예컨대 회계, 법률, 보험계리 등—의 장벽을 낮추고 보다 국제적으로 개방된 환경을 조성한다면, 그것이야말로 우리가 진정한 글로벌 중심지로 도약하는 길이자, 자유무역의 가치를 증명하는 방법이라고 생각합니다.

전광우 이사장: 좋은 질문과 답변 감사합니다. 이제 다음 질문을 받겠습니다. OECD 대사를 지낸 허경욱 대사님께서 질문하시겠습니다.

허경욱 대사: 매우 유익하고 훌륭한 발표에 감사드립니다. 저는 마지막으로 언급하신 "모든 사람을 공평하게 대하라"는 점을 바탕으로, 한 가지 관련된 질문을 드리고자 합니다. 이는 무역과 관세의 문제는 아니며, 대신 금융 분야에서의 최근 상황과 관련된 내용입니다. 특히, 미국의 트럼프 전 대통령 하에서 벌어지고 있는 여러 논의들에 대해 이야기하고자 합니다.

최근 '미란 보고서(Miran Report)'에 대한 논의가 많아지고 있습니다. 이 보고서를 쓴 스티븐 미란 미 백악관 경제자문위원

회(CEA) 위원장 같은 인물들이 '마러라고 환율 협정'과 같이 달러 약세를 위한 인위적 환율 협정 가능성을 계속해서 얘기해오고 있고, 국제적 영구채(international perpetual Treasury bond) 발행 등을 언급하고 있습니다. 일부는 이러한 관세 전쟁이 결국 이와 같은 금융 전략을 달성하기 위한 수단이라고 해석하고 있습니다.

영구 국채 발행과 환율 개입 메커니즘과 같은 견해들이 현실화될 가능성은 얼마나 될까요? 그리고 이러한 논의들이 글로벌 금융 시장과 국제 기관에 미칠 잠재적 영향은 무엇일까요?

마이클 마이넬리 박사: 대사님, 질문 감사합니다. 환율 문제나 그와 관련된 여러 이슈에 대해 이야기하자면, 우리는 항상 고전적인 삼자택일의 궁지(trilemma)에 놓이게 됩니다. 즉, 통화를 안정시키고 싶다면 자본 통제, 외환거래와 관련된 다양한 문제들이 복잡하게 얽히게 됩니다. 여러 번 논의된 것처럼, 이 궁지에서는 세 가지 요소 중 하나만 선택할 수 있습니다. 개인적으로 저는 자유로운 환율을 지지해왔고, 환율을 통제하려고 시도할 때마다 결국 실패했던 경험을 봤기 때문에 자유로운 환율을 지향하는 것이 맞다고 생각합니다. 외환 정책 같은 것들은 꼭 필요한 정책이지만, 항상 임시적인 것으로 보는 것이 바람직합니다.

그런데 제가 상당히 흥미롭게 생각하는 부분은 중앙은행 디지털화폐(CBDC)에 대한 논의입니다. 현재까지 중앙은행 디지털화폐를 도입하는 이유에 대해서는 명확한 답변이 많지 않았습니다. 예를 들어, 미국에서는 실리콘밸리 은행(SVB)을 보증하면서 사실상 중앙은행 디지털화폐가 도입되었다고 볼 수 있습니다. 이는 정부가 보증하는 화폐이지만, 실제로는 개인이 은행 계좌를 보유하고, 비자(Visa)社와 마스터카드(MasterCard)社의 송금 시스템이 복잡하게 얽혀 있는 상황입니다. 그러나 결국 이는 디지털화폐이며, 중앙은행이 이를 보증하고 있기 때문에 큰 문제가 되지 않는다고 볼 수 있습니다.

저는 인도의 중앙은행과 대화한 경험이 있고, 중국의 판공성 교수와도 이 문제에 대해 이야기를 나눈 적이 있습니다. 그런데 실험에 참여한 전문가들 역시 "왜 이런 것을 하고 있는지 잘 모르겠다"는 반응을 보입니다. 인도 중앙은행의 경우, 중소기업들이 "우리가 당신이 말하는 것을 이해할 수 없다"며 "무엇이 달라졌는지 모르겠다"는 의견을 계속해서 제시하고 있습니다. 다만 흥미로운 점은 사람들이 프로그래밍 가능한 화폐에 대해 이야기하기 시작했다는 것입니다.

그러나 프로그래밍 가능한 화폐에도 몇 가지 문제점이 존재합니다. 첫째, 정부에 세금 징수 능력을 매우 크게 부여할 수 있다는 점입니다. 예를 들어, 정부가 "서울 중심부에 가까워질수록 세율을 높이겠다"고 결정을 내린다면, 제주도에서는 세율이 0.01%이고 서울의 중심부에서는 99.99%로 올릴 수 있습니다. 물론 이런 세금은 매우 비합리적일 수 있지만, 정치인들이 중앙은행 디지털화폐를 통해 하루 만에 이런 세금을 만들 수 있다는 점에서 신중할 필요가 있습니다.

두 번째 문제는, 프로그래밍 가능한 화폐가 유동성을 해칠 수 있다는 것입니다. 하지만 중앙은행 디지털화폐가 가진 장점은 질문하신 것처럼, 우리가 동적인 통화 바스켓을 형성할 수 있다는 점입니다. 이는 그동안 매우 어려운 일이었고, 선박 운송이나 석유, 가스와 같은 클러스터에서 무역 통화를 만드는 일은 거의 불가능했습니다.

이제 우리는 여러 중앙은행의 통화로 구성된 에너지 코인 같은 바스켓을 통해 15년 동안 에너지를 구매하는 계약을 체결할 수 있게 될 것입니다. 이러한 변화는 제가 생각하는 미래의 방향을 보여주는 것이며, 환율 통제에 대한 제 생각을 약간 수정하게 만들 것입니다. 저는 이것이 앞으로 나아갈 길이라고 봅니다.

전광우 이사장: 답변 감사합니다. 이제 마지막 질문을 받겠습니다.

김진현 이사장: 매우 훌륭한 발표에 감사드립니다. 많은 것을 배웠습니다. 저는 오늘 강연 내용 중 법치주의에 대해 질문드리고자 합니다.

세상은 매우 빠르게 변화하고 있으며, 그와 함께 다양성도 급격히 증가하고 있습니다. 그러나 이러한 다양한 사회를 관리하고 하나로 모으는 능력은 감소하고 있는 것 같습니다. 유엔은 사실상 무력화되고 있으며, 안보리 상임이사국들은 중요한 사안에 대해 전혀 합의를 보지 못하고 있습니다. 뿐만 아니라, 각 국가의 리더십 품질과 역량이 과거에 비해 감소하고 있는 것 같습니다.

이러한 상황에서, 앞으로 어떻게 모든 발전하는 중심지들이 모여 평화롭게 협력할 수 있을까요? 감사합니다.

마이클 마이넬리 박사: 감사합니다. 간단히 답변 드리기에는 중요한 질문이라고 생각됩니다.

전 세계적으로 우리가 직면한 큰 문제 중 하나가 바로 거버넌스입니다. 그런데, 사실 4~5년마다 한 번씩 민주주의를 위해 투표하는 시스템이 더 많은 분열을 초래한 것으로 드러났습니다. 런던시장으로 재임할 당시, 사람들이 종종 "당신은 압도적인 다수로 선출되었는데, 그럼 당신의 의견은 무엇입니까?"라고 물었습니다. 저는 이렇게 답했습니다. "좋은 선거는 50.1%와 49.9%로 승리하는 것이 아닙니까?"

물론 "푸틴처럼 99%의 득표율을 얻는 독재자가 되고 싶지 않다"라는 의견도 이해하지만, 그럼에도 불구하고 사회가 향후 나아갈 방향에 대해 모두가 동의한다면, 그것이 나쁜 일일까요? 물론 99%는 과도한 숫자일 수 있지만, 65% 또는 70%의 득표율로 승리한 선거가 과연 문제가 될까요? 오히려 당파 정치가 우리 사회를 더 분열시키고 있는 측면이 있습니다. 다만, 이는 국가 차원에서의 이야기입니다.

지역 차원에서 보면, 우리는 새로운 기술을 보유하고 있음에도 불구하고, 이를 거버넌스 시스템에 어떻게 적용할지에 대해 여전히 답을 찾지 못하고 있습니다. 인류 역사상 복잡한 상황을 해결하는 방식으로는 고대 그리스의 토론, 법정에서의 판결 등이 있었습니다. 로마인들은 기원전 200년경, 대표 민주주의라는 중요한 제도를 도입했습니다.

그 이후 2,200년간 우리는 거버넌스를 근본적으로 재고해본 적이 거의 없습니다. 다만, 기본적인 투표 제도는 여전히 이어지고 있습니다. 이 문제는 매우 복잡하지만, 그럼에도 불구하고 무시되지 않고 있다는 점은 중요합니다. 예를 들어, 저는 지난해 사우디아라비아에서 이 문제에 대해 깊은 대화를 나눈 적이 있습니다. 그들은 어떻게 하면 왕정 체제를 유지하면서 바텀업 민주주의를 구현할 수 있을지 고민하고 있습니다. 가능성은 미지수이지만, 이러한 논의가 이루어지고 있다는 점은 흥미롭습니다.

또한 북유럽 국가들에서는 액체 민주주의(liquid democracy)라는 운동이 활발히 진행되고 있습니다. 이는 정책에 대한 투표에서 사람들이 이양 가능한 투표권을 갖게 하여, 예를 들어 환경 문제에 대한 전문가가 40,000표를, 해양 무역에 대한 전문가가 25,000표를 가지고 정책에 대해 투표하는 방식입니다. 이후 그 투표 결과는 정책 실행 여부를 결정하는 데 사용됩니다.

브라이언 이노(Brian Eno)라는 유명한 음악가는 UN과 협력하여 "One World or None" 프로젝트를 진행 중입니다. 작년에는 전 세계 시민을 대상으로 100명씩 무작위로 선정하여 시민 의회를 열었고, 흥미로운 점은 그 100명 중 절반이 여성이었으며, 80명의 통역사가 동원되었다는 사실입니다. 이는 영어 외에도 다양한 언어가 사용되었기 때문입니다. 그만큼 세계는 매우 다양하고 복잡합니다. 이 프로젝트는 결코 비웃음을 사기 위한 것이 아니라, 매우 혁신적이고 흥미로운 프로그램입니다.

결론적으로, 전 세계적으로 사람들은 바텀업 거버넌스를 어떻게 실현할지에 대해 많은 고민을 하고 있습니다. 만약 제게 또 다른 기회가 주어진다면, 새로운 거버넌스 구조를 연구하는 연구소를 설립해 보고 싶습니다. 다양한 제안들이 있지만, 로마 시대 이후로 거버넌스의 근본적인 방식에 대해서는 큰 발전이 없었던 것 같습니다.

전광우 이사장: 감사합니다. 오늘 저희와 함께 고견을 나눠주신 마이넬리 교수께 다시 한번 감사 말씀드립니다. 오늘 이 자리에 함께해 주신 모든 분들께도 감사드립니다.

Enhancing Korea's International Competitiveness: The Role of Finance in Times of Crisis

Michael Mainelli

Michael Mainelli

Dr. Michael Mainelli served as the 694th Lord Mayor of the City of London and is currently Chairman of the London Chamber of Commerce and of Z/Yen Group, a leading global think tank. He is an internationally recognized authority in finance, technology, and sustainability, having advised institutions such as the World Bank, the United Nations, and major financial regulators. He holds a PhD in Mathematics, Statistics, and Information Systems from the London School of Economics and a BA in Government with Physics, Mathematics, and Economics from Harvard University.

Opening Address

Jun Kwang-woo

Distinguished Guests, Ladies and Gentlemen,

It is with profound respect and pleasure that I welcome each one of you to IGE's Distinguished Forum. As we find ourselves navigating through the complexities of rapidly evolving global geopolitical landscape in this new era, marked notably by the onset of Trump 2.0, our assembly could not be more timely or crucial.

Korea has been recognized as a paragon of resilience and dynamism. Over decades marked by forward-looking innovation, policy-making, and global integration, Korea has ascended as a vanguard in technology, manufacturing, and international trade. Yet, history has consistently reminded us that crises-whether on a global scale, or within our own borders-present formidable challenges to our national credibility and competitive edge. It is our adeptness at coping with these turbulences that will solidify our long-term sustainable growth.

In this spirit, I am very pleased to introduce our esteemed speaker, the Honorable Dr. Michael Mainelli, former Lord Mayor of London and current Chairman of Z/Yen Group, and President of the London Chamber of Commerce and

Industry. Dr. Mainelli will share with us his invaluable insights on steering through these uncharted waters that we face today.

Ladies and gentlemen, please allow me to extend our deepest gratitude to His Excellency Dr. Chung Un Chan, former Prime Minister of Korea and President of Seoul National University, and the Honorable Mr. Oh Se-hoon, Mayor of Seoul Metropolitan City, for their congratulatory addresses. Moreover, I must express our profound appreciation to Mr. Ki-hak Sung, Chairman of Youngone Corporation, whose generous support of the IGE has been instrumental in making today's forum possible.

Thank you all very much.

Congratulatory Address

Chung Un Chan

Your Excellency Dr. Michael Mainelli, Distinguished Chairman Jun Kwang-woo, Honored Guests,

It is my great privilege to extend a heartfelt welcome and sincere gratitude to all of you for your presence at today's significant gathering.

I would like to extend particular appreciation to Dr. Mainelli for graciously traveling to Seoul during a time of considerable challenge for the Republic of Korea. Your visit is deeply meaningful, and the insights and wisdom you share with us today will serve as an invaluable bridge between Korea and the wider international community. We are confident that your perspectives will guide essential discourse on how Korea may navigate its current trials and further solidify its stature as a leading financial and economic center in East Asia.

The theme of this forum is both timely and of great consequence. Korea finds itself facing a confluence of challenges: persistent low growth and social polarization, political uncertainty at home, potential shifts in U.S. policy under a second Trump administration, and an increasingly complex geopolitical landscape. It is in such times that we are called not merely to endure difficulties, but to transform them into enduring opportunities.

To this end, I would like to offer three strategic imperatives that merit our shared attention and action.

First, Korea must reinforce its role as a global financial hub.

Seoul, in particular, possesses the attributes and potential to emerge as a preeminent financial center in Asia. Even in moments of volatility, Korea's financial sector must strive toward greater openness, innovation, and integration with global markets. By cultivating these strengths, we can foster deeper synergies across key industries and, in so doing, enhance Korea's international leadership and credibility, laying a firm foundation for sustainable, long-term growth.

Second, we must actively promote both the outward engagement of Korean enterprises and the inward flow of global investment.

The efforts of the financial sector, the business community, and especially the government—many of whom are represented here today—are essential. Korean firms must be empowered to pursue new opportunities abroad, while Korea must, in parallel, enhance its appeal as a destination for international capital. Our stable macroeconomic fundamentals and advanced industrial capacity position

Korea as a compelling and trustworthy partner in the global economy. Continued efforts by the government to improve the investment climate—through regulatory reform, support for innovation, and a commitment to sustainability—are imperative.

Third, in this era of digital transformation, Korea—renowned as a global leader in IT—must actively attract international business and investment.

Our nation's technological capabilities, particularly in the fields of information and communication technology, are among the finest in the world. We must now harness these capabilities to position Korea as a strategic base for global enterprises seeking to expand across Asia. Seoul, in particular, is emerging as a dynamic ecosystem where cutting-edge startups and technology firms can flourish. We must do more to share this vision with the world and to build a policy and investment environment that invites global participation in Korea's future.

Dr. Mainelli, I trust that your visit will offer a meaningful opportunity for Korea to further elevate its image and presence on the global stage. Through your distinguished global network—including London and other key centers of influence—I am confident that Korea's reputation as a trusted and forward-looking nation will be further strengthened. May this forum serve as an important milestone in that ongoing journey.

As we look ahead, Korea will continue to strive toward its role as a dynamic and trusted financial power—driven by innovation, resilience, and global cooperation. I look forward to working with all of you gathered here today in building a stronger, more prosperous future for the Republic of Korea. Thank you.

Keynote Speech
Michael Mainelli

Ladies and Gentlemen,

Good morning. It is a true pleasure and an honor for me to be here with you today.

First and foremost, I would like to express my gratitude to the Institute for Global Economics(IGE) for graciously hosting today's event and for their generous support of my visit to Korea. My sincere thanks go to Chairman Jun Kwang-woo and all the members of the IGE team for their warm hospitality and dedication.

I would also like to extend my sincere appreciation to Youngone Corporation for their generous support of today's forum. The title of my keynote today is "Connectivity and Cities." In a time marked by uncertainty and fragmentation, bringing people together and fostering meaningful connections is no easy task. Yet, I firmly believe that such efforts lead to profoundly positive outcomes. I am truly grateful for the support that has made it possible for this important gathering to take place during such a challenging period, both at home and abroad.

Today, I have been invited to speak on how Korea can

strengthen its standing as a global hub and enhance its international credibility, particularly at a time when domestic political risks are at an unprecedented high and external uncertainties-ranging from the inauguration of a second Trump administration to ongoing global conflicts-are mounting. To this end, I will share insights drawn primarily from the research conducted by my organization, Z/Yen Group. Toward the end of my presentation, I will also offer a brief reflection on my experiences serving as the Lord Mayor of London last year, and some of the lessons I have taken from that role.

At Z/Yen Group, we began exploring issues related to urban development back in the late 1990s. One of the driving forces behind our research was the UK's decision not to join the eurozone. At the time, there were widespread concerns that London might suffer economically as a result. We published a report in 2002 titled Sizing Up the City, which examined London's global competitors-cities like New York, Paris, and Frankfurt. In hindsight, it was not a very good report. It missed several critical players on the global stage, even then-Tokyo, Dubai, Hong Kong, Singapore, to name just a few.

This led us to initiate three major studies, the first of which is the Global Financial Centres Index (GFCI). Just last week, we released the 37th edition of that index.

Today, I'd like to explore a few key themes: What do we

mean by "commercial centers", which encompass more than just financial hubs? Why are networks and connectivity so important? How do we measure these factors? I'll also share a few thoughts on Seoul's current position, and conclude with reflections on what makes a center successful.

Successful centers are all about interaction. The renowned economist Jane Jacobs, who conducted pioneering work on urban development, emphasized that cities are co-created by people. At their core, cities are about people coming together-and the greatest enabler of that is connectivity. Whether through air travel, cultural events, logistics, or maritime infrastructure, cities thrive when people and ideas flow freely.

These urban centers typically draw together three key groups: investors, traders, and what I like to call "guarantors"-a broad category that includes accountants, credit rating agencies, lawyers, and others who help ensure systems function properly. Supporting these core groups is a broader network of professionals: regulators, consultants, actuaries, scientists, engineers, and more. In essence, commercial centers are clusters of expertise-places where people want to meet, exchange ideas, and do business.

What is the vision for such centers? In London, we have been building from the ground up to foster interaction. One of the concepts we embrace is "serendipity"-those chance encounters that lead to exciting, innovative developments. We believe that creating environments where such moments can occur is essential to nurturing a vibrant, successful city.

In the City of London, I've been part of a group-actually leading it-focused on what we call "groundage," a program aimed at reclaiming urban space and allowing people to move through the city more freely. This initiative began roughly 15 years ago, and we're now starting to see its benefits. For those of you who've been to London, you may have noticed you can now walk through the Bloomberg Center-something that was not possible just eight years ago.

At that time, the entire area was blocked off to pedestrians. There's a saying that "22 bishops gave, 100 bishops gave," and so on-we're essentially trying to create more opportunities for serendipity.

In a similar spirit, we've launched a program called "Roofage," which aims to open up rooftops across the city. There are now around eight publicly accessible rooftop spaces where people can gather freely and enjoy the view. These small changes collectively amount to something significant.

Another notable trend in commercial centers is the shift away from dependence on single industries. In the past, cities often grew around one defining industry-mining towns, or cities built around water and power infrastructure, for example.

Today, however, cities increasingly share a similar vision.

You could hand the same strategy template to nearly any mayor: inclusivity, innovation, smart infrastructure, digital advancement, environmental sustainability, high quality of life, and resilience. As a result, it's becoming harder to distinguish one city from another.

Most modern cities now revolve around three major domains: science and technology, economics and finance, and logistics. You can particularly see this pattern in mainland China over the last 30 years, where many cities have developed along strikingly similar lines.

My theme as Lord Mayor last year was "Connect to Prosper." I aimed to emphasize the importance of connectivity—among people, systems, and knowledge flows. We sought to celebrate the exchange of ideas and expertise that moves through London and extends globally, linking us with cities like Seoul and Busan.

To illustrate this, I often used the analogy of the coffeehouse. Perhaps in Korea, a teahouse might resonate more, but the point remains. When coffeehouses first emerged in the mid-1600s, they were known as "penny universities." For the price of a penny, one could sit all day, drink coffee, and engage in conversations with people from all walks of life—treated as equals. Incidentally, in English, the phrase "spend a penny" is a euphemism for using the toilet, but here, it truly referred to buying a day's worth of intellectual exchange.

It was within these coffeehouses that major institutions were born. Stock trading agreements were made over coffee. Lloyd's of London, the insurance market, originated in such a setting. The Baltic Exchange, which facilitated maritime trade, also came out of the Baltic Coffeehouse.

Networks like these are fascinating to scientists because they illustrate how intricate and dynamic life can be. Networks matter because they form the foundational structure for almost all systems. Life itself is built upon interconnected nodes. Even artificial intelligence—so widely discussed today—is essentially a network of connections within a neural framework.

Network science reveals a great deal about complexity. For example, network boundaries are rarely clear-cut. Take a city map—it's full of connections, but often ambiguous in how those connections are defined.

So what defines a city? Its defensive walls, like London's medieval walls? Its planning regulations, tax policies, the location of workers and residents? Or is it its infrastructure—air, water, sea transport, waste systems? The answer is: it's all of the above. Cities are complex ecosystems.

Even a seemingly simple question like "What is the population of the city?" becomes complicated. The City of London, for instance, has only about 8,000 residents within its one square mile, but it hosts approximately 687,000 daily workers. That's why we were hit particularly hard by COVID—without commuters, the city struggled. But when operating normally, the City of London is more densely concentrated than Manhattan, which spreads around 350,000 people across six square miles. In some ways, we're even more intense than Tokyo, although Tokyo handles greater volumes, dispersed across multiple centers.

In the City of London, everyone is there for business. No one is simply walking the dog or popping out for a pint of milk. This leads to a very distinctive culture—one that values hyper-punctuality and efficiency. It's not uncommon for a 25-year-old to strike up a conversation in a pub by asking, "What do you do for a living?"—because that's what everyone is there for.

This is why network analysis is both crucial and challenging. While science can model networks—for instance, by inverting nodes and links—it often falls short. We still need art, intuition, and strategic thinking to fully understand these systems.

One concept in network science is "emergent properties"— a technical term for surprises. Networks often behave in unexpected ways. Who would have imagined that a network of neurons connected by synapses could lead to consciousness?

From networks, we observe surprising phenomena: order,

responsiveness, growth, regulation, adaptation, and even evolution. According to Béla Suki, biological complexity as we know it could not have evolved without networks. Networks adapt to shocks—and sometimes even thrive from them.

So how do we analyze these complex systems? We began with the concept of connectivity. One of our tools is a chart that visualizes how professionals rate various cities, offering insights into where business is happening. When we began in the 1990s, we started with London's local network—not just in finance, but across disciplines.

One chart showed the following within a two-mile radius of the Guildhall: 40 learned societies (in blue), 70 universities (in red), and 130 research institutes. This intense concentration is often overlooked. London is not only a financial center—it is about 35–40% financial and professional services, and around 35% science and research. Many forget that we are also the historical home of the Royal Society of Science, dating back to the 15th through 17th centuries. In addition, London plays a central role in media, culture, and education.

We began to explore factor assessment indices. This approach combines perception-based and empirical data to create a predictive model for assessing city competitiveness. We survey roughly 5,000 professionals every six months, asking them to rate 130 cities. These results are then correlated with about 130 instrumental factors. This allows us to estimate how someone might rate a city they've never visited.

I've taken the survey myself. Based on your preferences—your profession, lifestyle, family status, recreational interests—the model can predict your rating of a city with surprising accuracy. While it's not exactly artificial intelligence, we use support vector machines, a machine learning technique, to make these predictions. It turns perception into measurable insight.

Where do we stand? Our world, as depicted in the Global Financial Centers Index (GFCI), looks like this. When we first started publishing in 2005, 2006, and 2007, we initially tracked 46 financial centers. Today, as I mentioned, we are monitoring well over 140 centers. Some may think this increase is due to lowering our standards. In reality, that's not the case. What we are witnessing is a proliferation of financial centers. I'll revisit this point shortly.

You're likely wondering where Seoul stands in this context. The results from last week focused primarily on the top 20 centers. As the mayor and others have pointed out, Seoul has been performing extremely well. However, Seoul wasn't even on this chart 20 years ago, so the progress made is truly remarkable. Please take a moment to give yourselves a round of applause – it's a job well done.

That being said, I am aware that here in Korea, you're accustomed to aiming for the top 1, 2, or even 3 positions in many industries. So, I agree with the mayor's sentiment that there is still much potential for growth, though it will likely require some radical changes. You're reaching the upper limits of what's achievable with the current approach.

I would also like to mention Busan. We don't just analyze it as a standalone city, but it currently ranks at number 25. Considering that it ranked 51st just a decade ago, this progress is truly remarkable. It demonstrates that with clear determination and focused effort, significant transformation is indeed possible. This illustrates how significant progress can be made when there is a clear focus and determination.

Now, let's take a look at some other key trends. What are the long-term developments shaping the landscape?

One of the most significant long-term trends has been the rise of "Asia". When we launched the index, many people were skeptical, saying there was no way Seoul, Beijing, or Shanghai would ever become global financial centers. This was only 20 years ago, and frankly, it was probably only about 10 years ago that these cities started to make a mark.

I've also been criticized for having too many respondents from Asia completing our surveys. Over 50% of the respondents are from Asia, to which I respond that, at present, around 60% of global finance is located in Asia. So, we still have work to do in terms of diversifying our respondent pool to better reflect this shift.

Another key point is that you should never rely solely on one number. The further down the ranking you are, the more important it is to assess the depth and breadth of a city's performance. We use a method to rank cities based on their competitive profiles. If we look at the chart here, it shows rankings across 12 different categories—international, regional, and global. Again, Seoul performs very well in these rankings.

In the early days, Seoul was seen mainly as a regional center. However, it has steadily expanded its influence over time. Another useful approach is to break down performance across various sectors. If you're truly aiming to analyze a center's position, simply saying, "we are ranked number 10" isn't enough, just as it doesn't help to say, "my football team wins 47% of the time." You need to understand what each player is doing, how the team works together, and whether the strategies being used are effective. Success requires proficiency across multiple areas.

When we look at the data across different sectors, we see how leading players are positioned. Seoul's performance, highlighted in blue, shows that it wouldn't be ranked number 10 without excelling in many different sectors. This will become increasingly important. When a city is successful, it has to excel in many different categories simultaneously, and those strengths reinforce each other. Success is built on a foundation of achievements in multiple areas.

The second area we are focusing on, which is particularly interesting, is FinTech.

Seoul has performed exceptionally well in this domain, and I believe this could become a core element of your competitive advantage, especially given the strong IT skills present across Korea, including in Seoul and Busan.

However, I would like to highlight something: as a technologist myself, who first entered the finance sector in the early 1980s to introduce computers into finance, FinTech is not a new concept. In fact, this is something I have been involved in throughout my career—digitizing finance.

What we have achieved so far is that finance has become highly digitized, and this has had a significant impact on the structures of banks and insurance companies, which are now increasingly automated. However, one thing that remains is the lack of integration between finance and the real economy.

You might recall that, 17 years ago during the financial crisis, there were widespread complaints that finance was not truly supporting the real economy. Even today, when we look at industries like shipping and aviation, we find that, despite the impressive systems in place, these industries face challenges when they attempt to transition into finance, such as issuing invoices or processing payments. These processes are far from seamless.

What I hope to see is the evolution of finance into more API-based models, where services are purchased as needed. We also need to make significant progress on microfinance—the ability to process very small payments effectively, such as letters of credit or credit lines, which we've been talking about for over 40 years. There's still much work to be done to integrate finance more effectively with the real economy, an area in which we have not yet succeeded.

In London, for example, we launched the Smart Economies Network program two years ago, aiming to create a digital verification system for individuals and companies globally. This system combines the Nordic XROAD framework, used by governments, and applies it to trade. We've published four reports on what can be done, with one report focusing on digital verification published just last week.

We are also looking at competitive factors across various regions, and once again, Seoul stands out as performing exceptionally well. One aspect that is particularly encouraging is the strength of your regulatory system, which is viewed globally as robust, providing you with a solid foundation for further progress.

Now, I'd like to quickly address the question of whether your city is stable or dynamic. We assess cities based on the volatility of their factors and how much influence they have over these factors.

A city that is too unstable, found in the top right corner of our chart, is one to avoid. However, stability in the bottom left corner is also not ideal, as it implies little ability to adapt or maneuver. I believe Seoul is in an excellent position—well-placed to make changes and have a substantial impact without being stagnant.

It's also important to note that our analysis isn't solely focused on finance. We also run the Smart Centers Index, which evaluates approximately 77 centers. Looking at the top 15 cities in Asia, Seoul is positioned very well.

In addition, we have an index that evaluates environmental sustainability. Based on my recent research, I believe this is an area where Korea could improve. Specifically, I'm referring to carbon trading and broader emission reduction efforts. This is a challenging issue, given Korea's heavy industry, and though progress has been made, it seems that more action is needed in this regard.

In the Global Green Finance Index (GGFI), we track 97 centers based on their environmental performance. In Asia Pacific, Seoul performs well, but on a global scale, there is room for improvement. With the global push towards sustainability, especially in the financial and scientific sectors, it's clear that there is a growing confluence between success in finance and green initiatives.

It's not surprising that cities that are seen as green and

responsible attract a lot of interest. For instance, countries like Chile, Uruguay, and Thailand have issued sovereign sustainability-linked bonds, where interest rates increase if green targets are not met. This approach is exciting because it holds governments accountable to their long-term commitments, which is particularly important in the renewable energy sector, where investors need to make 25-year commitments.

Our index allows us to examine whether centers are accurately rated. We can assess a center's performance without revealing its name.

On a thousand-point scale, Seoul performs well within the global financial centers, with its ratings aligning with its standing. For Busan, however, the rating is slightly negative, but still very close to where it should be.

However, when it comes to the Smart Centers Index, Seoul scores 165 points lower than its reputation index. There is a significant opportunity here for Seoul to improve its marketing as an IT and finance hub. More effort is needed to communicate Seoul's strengths in these areas.

As for environmental sustainability, as I mentioned earlier, Seoul is overrated by 49 points, indicating that more action is required to match the city's green aspirations with real results.

Finally, I'd like to touch on regulation. While regulation is a critical factor in building a financial center, it follows a U-curve model. There can be too much regulation, just as there can be too little. Balancing regulation properly is key to maintaining a thriving financial ecosystem.

We've seen this struggle in areas like digital assets, and I think we're going to see it in AI as well. AI regulation is coming, and over the past two years in the City of London, we've run a program encouraging the global financial services industry to use ISO 42001 as the regulatory approach to artificial intelligence.

If we can establish a single certification passport, much like we do in finance with ISO 20022 for international payments or ISO 27000 and 65000 for risk and security, we can avoid a plethora of competing regulations. This would prevent a situation where, in order to export your services, you'd find yourself having to meet a variety of inconsistent regulatory requirements. In fact, at the moment, over half of the U.S. states require you to meet specific AI regulations just for insurance, and it's the same for the EU.

I was pleased this week to find that South Korea's regulatory approach to AI has been relatively relaxed, and I think that's the right approach. But there are market-based solutions, through the International Standards Organization (ISO), that would allow the industry to avoid trade barriers caused by AI regulation.

As I move towards concluding, let me share a few thoughts. There are a wide range of emerging digital opportunities, but most centers around the world could do all of those. As I mentioned earlier, it's becoming harder to differentiate between commercial centers, and it's becoming harder to differentiate between financial centers as well.

But just last week, while traveling through China on similar research, one thing stood out: the Chinese are very focused on numbers. So, I will conclude with four lessons, seven wishes, and one fundamental strategy, if I may.

What are the four lessons? Well, when you're the head of the world's oldest democratic workers' and residents' cooperative, as we are in the City of London—workers have had the vote since about 640 AD, so we're nearly 1,400 years old—you gain a very different perspective on life. You truly look to the long term. Over the years, we've learned four key lessons, and after reading my history, I believe I can substantiate these lessons quite well.

The first is defense. This is certainly one of the big lessons. We in the West often forget this, but it's become more apparent with Ukraine. I am conscious that here in South Korea, you've never forgotten that, and it's crucial when considering issues such as capital controls. These are very real and important issues. No one brings their money to a war zone—that's a fundamental fact of life. But once you have defense in place, you can move on.

The second lesson is what I would call the rule of law, though it's a much broader concept. It's not just about litigation. Yes, it involves fair courts and equal treatment under the law, but it also encompasses the entire culture of the place. Does the venue foster trust? Can I trust people to do things? Because, ideally, I don't want to go to court. The courts are a last resort.

What matters is the availability of alternative mechanisms—arbitration, mediation, conciliation, expert determination. These are all things we understand in financial services, but sometimes we forget that the rule of law is central to everything. I'm conscious that you're going through some challenges at the moment. We've faced similar challenges in the UK. With Boris Johnson, we had the prorogation of Parliament, and our judges were attacked and insulted. We see what's going on in America right now. But, as you well know, engaging with these challenges at your peril is risky. The rule of law is fundamental to everything we do.

The third lesson is that open trade is key. You have to support open trade for long-term economic success. The fourth is the need for access to skills and talent. These are the four lessons we've learned.

As for the seven wishes, I've already shown them to you, and they align with what I've discussed. These are all things that South Korea can follow and implement. But I think the most important thing to remember is the connectivity diagram. In this diagram, Seoul is right at the core of what works. You can see how well you're doing, but if you want to succeed, I wouldn't measure success by ranking yourself as number 10, number 9, number 8, or so on. Instead, if you measure your connectivity, the results in the GFCI and the Smart Centers Index will prove themselves.

So, where do we end? Well, as I move to one fundamental strategy, I just want to point out that connectivity is everything. You have to be connected to be a commercial center. You cannot be an international commercial center without international people. And you've made great strides in being welcoming to overseas talent. I remember coming here when the signs weren't even in English. There are so many things you've done to improve that, and it's a credit to you.

Successful people want to live in successful cosmopolitan cities. I was explaining this at breakfast and in other meetings today: do not underestimate the impact of K-culture globally. K-pop, K-drama—these have made a huge impact. People who had never heard of Korea are now discovering it through Netflix, absorbing Korean culture. Korean court dramas are a big thing, too, which demonstrate respect for the rule of law in a way that Westerners can understand. Your reputation is vital—it's something you can build, but you can also lose it overnight.

So, what is the one fundamental strategy for success? It's a very simple one: treat all commerce fairly. That's it. Open up your center, ensure it's well defended, and guarantee that everyone is treated fairly. When you do this, you'll have a successful financial center. There are nuances to this, of course. It goes beyond just telling your regulators to be fair. There are subtleties to this. It goes well beyond telling your regulators to be fair on it.

Take, for example, something as simple as competition regulation. One of our weakest areas in the United Kingdom is our retail banking. We have one of the worst retail banking systems in the world. Which is surprising because we have, in my opinion, perhaps the finest wholesale finance in the world. But three banks control over 70% of the industry. Four banks control, I think, 82%. That's not very competitive. And is that a market that you want to enter as a foreign retail bank? No. Do you have any problems?

So what you want to see is a whole variety. You don't want one giant pension fund. You want to see competition. If I enter a market where there's one giant pension fund as a foreign entity and I begin to have a problem, we know who's going to win. And it's not me. So I stay out of those waters. And just as a point of fact, the city of London, that one square mile, has 24,000 businesses. 40% of FX trading. 95% of protection and indemnity, mutual insurance. I could go on and on. I was the Lord Mayor, so that's what I was selling.

But the truth is, of those 24,000 businesses, 23,750 are small and medium-sized enterprises. We only have 250 organizations, over 500 people. And it's all these small businesses that control that huge wholesale market, which is often missed because the signs are there. Morgan Stanley, Goldman Sachs, J.P. Morgan. That's not the real business. The real business in the wholesale market is actually in the SMEs.

And those 687,000 workers are up since Brexit. Brexit was in 2016. At that time, we had 525,000 workers. Why do we know so clearly? Because they had the vote. We did our next vote on it just in November, and it was 687,000.

And for those of you who are cynical, they're not all working in compliance. Of that, global assets under management have grown from 11% to 13% over that same eight-year period. So we are very, very competitive, because people believe they will be treated fairly in London.

And I might argue that I was not pro-Brexit, and still am not, but that our disappearance from Europe has made people feel they might not be treated quite as fairly in Frankfurt or Paris, and they might as well base their European operations in London. So we're doing fine at that level. The UK, as a nation, is a more complex beast.

But the one fundamental strategy for success remains: show that you will treat everyone fairly. Indicators like the number of businesses and the variety within sectors—rather than a single giant entity—are signs of a healthy and successful market.

Thank you so much for listening this morning. I also want to thank all of you for coming out early. I appreciate your presence and the effort you've made. I'd also like to extend my thanks to my hosts, especially the Institute for Global Economics, for helping with my research. And thank you to Youngone Group for sponsoring this event.

Q&A Session

Jun Kwang-woo: Thank you very much, Dr. Mainelli, for your illuminating presentation. Continuing with our long tradition of engaging the floor in dialogue, I would now like to invite a question or two from the audience. First, Ambassador Ahn Ho-Young. Former Korea's ambassador to the United States and to the European Union.

Ahn Ho-Young: Lord Mayer, such a pleasure and honor.

In your last slide, you mentioned treating all commerce equally. This concept seems similar to the principle of Most Favored Nation(MFN) in international trade. Considering what Mr. Trump is doing in the United States, where he is essentially dismantling the principle of MFN, I began to wonder: is this not only a matter of trade, but also an attack on the broader system of rule of law?

I would very much like to hear your thoughts on this. Thank you.

Michael Mainelli: Well, firstly, Your Excellency, thank you for your kind remarks. I was actually, my guild, we have guilds in London, and I was master of the Worshipful Company of World Traders. And we've done quite a bit of research on trade as well. In particular, where trade flows were known. Tariffs. Well, tariffs are an interesting problem.

In 1973, Britain decided to join the EU. And if you talk to Australians or New Zealanders, as far as they're concerned, we kicked them in the teeth. They were exporting lamb to Britain, and we said, we can't take your lamb any longer. Now we're in the EU. Tough on you.

Now, I happened to have met the Australian High Commissioner at that time. And interestingly, his son was High Commissioner at the time of Brexit. An interesting bit of nepotism, perhaps. But in truth, he pointed out that we Australians got going.

And I said, what do you mean? He said, we just went to people and we said, we'd love all of your cheap subsidised trade goods. Please, keep sending them to us. We don't mind. By the way, if you'd like to buy any of our stuff, that's fine. And as you'll be aware, Australia signed more free trade agreements than any nation on earth.

And it did it with a department of less than 350 people. And that's because they really took free trade seriously. Now, I know that they're not perfect. I have. Nobody is. But I look at this, and those of us in the West, I think, face a couple of issues.

If Mr. Trump is so wrong about tariffs, and I believe that intellectually, and I believe in the sense of not treating others fairly, then shouldn't we look at this as a giant global experiment? And those of us who are not are going far harder towards free trade. So I think some of the challenges facing us are going to be what do we do with the CPTPP. Comprehensive and Progressive Treaty.

So what if we all decide to move towards free trade assertively and aggressively to really drop it? What if here, in Seoul, in services, particularly in accounting, legal, actuarial, you start dropping some of those, making yourselves even more international, even more open? I think that would be the best way to prove Mr. Trump wrong, in my view.

Jun Kwang-woo: Thank you. Now, let's move on to the next question. Ambassador Hur Kyungwook, former Ambassador to the OECD, is with us today.

Hur Kyungwook: Thank you very much for your very informative and excellent presentation.

I would like to follow up on your final point—about treating everyone fairly—by raising a related issue, not on the trade and tariff side, but rather in the realm of finance, particularly in the context of ongoing developments in the United States under former President Trump.

There has been growing discussion around the so-called "Miran Report." When people refer to this, they often allude to figures like the Chair of the Council of Economic Advisers, who has reportedly mentioned concepts such as the "Mar-a-Lago exchange rate accord" and even floated the idea of introducing a kind of international perpetual Treasury bond. Some interpret these developments as part of a broader financial strategy, suggesting that the current tariff wars may, in fact, be a means to advance this agenda.

In your view, how realistic are these proposals-such as perpetual bond issuance and exchange rate intervention mechanisms-and what potential impact might they have on global financial markets and institutions?

Michael Mainelli: Your Excellency, it is a pleasure to see that you haven't lost any of your ambassadorial talent, which sadly, we often do. I've always been impressed with how ambassadors manage to remain calm and composed, even when I would be losing my temper. You, however, maintain a great deal of poise.

Now, regarding your question about exchange rates and related issues, we are faced with that classic trilemma: if you want to maintain a stable currency, if you want to impose capital controls, and if you want to allow for foreign entry, it's a complex issue. As has been argued many times before, you can only achieve one of the three elements in the trilemma. Personally, I've always been in favor of free exchange rates. I think every time we've tried to control exchange rates, it has gone awry. So, policies like foreign controls are essential, but they should always be seen as temporary.

One thing that excites me, however, is the development

of central bank digital currencies (CBDCs). So far, the arguments for them have been unclear. The United States has, in effect, already implemented a CBDC through the guarantee provided for Silicon Valley Bank. Essentially, it is a government-backed currency; it's just that your bank account is held privately, and the interbank process is clumsy. But in principle, it's a digital currency that is guaranteed by the central bank, so what's the real issue?

I've spoken with the Reserve Bank of India and Professor Pan Gongsheng in China about these experiments, and while they all acknowledge the potential, they are still uncertain about the ultimate purpose. For instance, customers at the Reserve Bank of India's SME sector say they don't understand the difference between CBDCs and existing systems.

One exciting idea with CBDCs is programmable money. However, there are challenges with this as well. For example, governments would have massive tax powers. A politician could create a highly variable tax system, targeting specific regions with extreme variations based on proximity to the capital. This could be done in a matter of hours with a CBDC, and though it may seem appealing, we must be cautious.

Despite these concerns, CBDCs could help form dynamic trade baskets of currencies, which has always been difficult. For example, we could create a currency basket tied to energy contracts, adjusting based on GDP. These are some of the exciting possibilities that could emerge from this technology.

This may challenge my previous views on controlling exchange rates, but I now see this as the way forward.

Jun Kwang-woo: Thank you for your insightful response. We will now move on to the final question.

Kim Chinhyun: Thank you, Dr. Mainelli, for your excellent presentation. I have gained so much insight this morning. When you spoke about the strength of the City of London, you began with the first point, the rule of law, which leads me to my question.

The world is changing at an unprecedented pace, and along with that change, it is becoming increasingly diverse. However, in contrast, the ability to govern these diverse societies and bring them together seems to be diminishing. The United Nations, for example, appears to be losing its influence, with the five permanent members of the Security Council, each holding veto power, unable to reach agreement on any significant issue.

Moreover, I believe that, in my personal view, the quality of leadership and the capacity to govern, if anything, seems to be diminishing compared to the past. How do you envision the future, where we can bring together all these emerging centers of power and work toward peaceful cooperation? Thank you.

Michael Mainelli: Thank you. It is always difficult for me to provide a brief response, especially to such a thought-provoking question. If I may say so, I believe we are globally struggling with governance.

The concept of holding a vote every four or five years as part of a democracy has actually proven to be quite divisive. One of the challenges I faced in the City was when people would say, "Well, as Lord Mayor, you were elected by an overwhelming majority," and I would respond, "So, what is your opinion on this matter?"

A "good" election might be one where a candidate wins by 50.1% over 49.9%. But people would object, stating that they didn't want to be like some autocrat, like Putin, who wins with 99%. I would counter, asking, "What is wrong with that? If society genuinely agrees on the direction forward, shouldn't that be a positive outcome?"

Now, I understand that a 99% win may be somewhat absurd, but what is wrong with a 65% or 70% majority? In some ways, party politics has become divisive, but that is more of an issue at the national level.

When we look at the local level, despite the new technologies we have, we have yet to find ways to effectively deploy them within our governance systems. If we reflect on the history of humanity and its attempts to extract narratives from complex situations, we see the Greeks with their debates, the Romans with their tribunals, and court cases where people have tried to determine what should be done. The Romans introduced a major innovation around 200 BC—representative democracy.

However, since then, we have had over 2,200 years, and we have not truly rethought how we approach governance, aside from the basic principle of voting. This is a challenging area, but it is not being ignored. Interestingly, I had an extended discussion on this topic last year in Saudi Arabia, where they are trying to figure out how to implement a bottom-up democratic system of governance while retaining a monarchy. I am not claiming that this is achievable, but they are actively having those discussions.

In the Nordic countries, there is a movement known as "Liquid Democracy," which seeks to vote on policies and allows people to transfer their votes. So, for example, at a party meeting, I, as an expert on environmental issues, might have 40,000 votes, while you, as an expert on maritime trade, have 25,000 votes, and together we vote on a policy.

That vote is then translated into a decision on whether or not to proceed. This approach is still in the early stages, but it is an intriguing model. Brian Eno, the musician, has been working on a project with the United Nations called One World or None.

Last year, they conducted a global citizens' assembly,

randomly selecting 100 people. It was an interesting assembly because, of the 100 participants, 50% were women—something I don't fully understand, but that was the case. They also required 80 translators because the discussions weren't solely in English. It's a reminder of how vast and diverse the world is. However, the purpose here is not to make light of it, but to highlight the exciting nature of the program.

What I am pointing out is that people around the world are grappling with how to establish bottom-up governance, and if I had another life, I would likely want to contribute to setting up an institute dedicated to exploring new governance structures and their potential effectiveness. Many proposals exist, but we have yet to progress significantly beyond the Roman era.

Jun Kwang-woo: Thank you very much. Please join me in expressing our sincere gratitude to Dr. Mainelli for his exceptional insights shared with us today. Thank you once again.

세계경제연구원 특별강연
간행물 목록

IGE Publications

Occasional Paper Series

1993

	Title	Author
93-01	Clintonomics and the New World Order: Implications for Korea-US Relations	C. Fred Bergsten
93-02	The Uruguay Round, NAFTA and US-Korea Economic Relations	Jeffrey Schott

1994

	Title	Author
94-01	Korea in the World: Today and Tomorrow	Paul Kennedy
94-02	US-Japan Technological Competition and Implications for Korea	Ronald A. Morse
94-03	The Problems of the Japanese Economy and their Implications for Korea	Toyoo Gyohten
94-04	Changing US and World Economies and their Market Prospects	Allen Sinai
94-05	Prospects for New World Monetary System and Implications for Korea	John Williamson
94-06	The Promises of the WTO for the Trading Community	Arthur Dunkel

1995

	Title	Author
95-01	Mexican Peso Crisis and its Implications for the Global Financial Market	Charles H. Dallara
95-02	The World Economic Trend and US Economic Outlook	Allen Sinai
95-03	New Games, New Rules, and New Strategies	Lester Thurow
95-04	The United States and North Korea Future Prospects	Robert Scalapino
95-05	US Foreign Policy toward East Asia and the Korean Peninsula	James A. Baker III
95-06	US Trade Tension with Japan and their Implications for Korea	Anne O. Krueger
95-07	Prospects for Northeast Asian Economic Development: Japan's Perspective	Hisao Kanamori

1996

	Title	Author
96-01	Trends of International Financial Market and Prospects of Global Economy in 1996	Allen Sinai
96-02	Future European Model: Economic Internationalization and Cultural Decentralization	Jørgen Ørstrøm Møller
96-03	Evolving Role of the OECD in the Global Economy	Donald Johnston
96-04	The Political Context and Consequences of East Asian Economic Growth	Francis Fukuyama
96-05	Korea's New Global Responsibilities	A. W. Clausen

1997

	Title	Author
97-01	East Asia in Overdrive: Multinationals and East Asian Integration	Wendy Dobson
97-02	American Security Policy in the Asia Pacific - Three Crisis and How We Dealt with Them	William Perry
97-03	Public Sector Reform in New Zealand and its Relevance to Korea	Donald Hunn

1998

	Title	Author
98-01	Global Cooperations and National Government: Why We Need Multilateral Agreement on Investment	Edward Graham
98-02	Korean-American Relations: The Search for Stability at a Time of Change	W. Anthony Lake
98-03	Korea: From Vortex to Hub of Northeast Asia	Donald P. Gregg
98-04	German Unification: Economic Consequences and Policy Lessons	Juergen B. Donges
98-05	Globalization and versus Tribalization: The Dilemma at the End of the 20th Century	Guy Sorman

1999

	Title	Author
99-01	Economic and Political Situation in North Korea and Security in Northeast Asia	Marcus Noland
99-02	The International Financial Market and the US Dollar/Yen Exchange Rate: An Overview and Prospects for the Future	Kenneth S. Courtis

	Title	Author
99-03	Prospects and Policy Recommendations for the Korean Economy and Other Asian Economies	Donald Johnston/ Hubert Neiss
99-04	Reflections on Contrasting Present-day US and Japanese Economic Performances	Hugh Patrick
99-05	Challenge for the World Economy: Where Do the Risks Lie?	Rudiger Dornbusch

2000

	Title	Author
00-01	North Korea-US Relationship: Its Current Condition and Future Prospects	Stephen W. Bosworth
00-02	Global New Economy: Challenges and Opportunities for Korea	Soogil Young
00-03	Global Trend in Financial Supervision	YongKeun Lee
00-04	Asia Grows, Japan Slows: Prospects for the World Economy and Markets	Kenneth S. Courtis
00-05	The Future of International Financial System and its Implications for Korea	Morris Goldstein
00-06	Prospects for Millennium Round Trade Negotiations and Korea-US Free Trade Agreement	Jeffrey Schott/ InBeom Choi
00-07	Prospects for the Multilateral Economic Institutions	Anne O. Krueger
00-08	Avoiding Apocalypse: The Future of the Two Koreas	Marcus Noland
00-09	Attracting FDI in the Knowledge Era	Andrew Fraser
00-10	The Economic and Foreign Policies of the New US Administration and Congress	C. Fred Bergsten
00-11	Korea and the US: Partners in Prosperity and Security	Stephen W. Bosworth
00-12	The Outlook for Asia and Other Emerging Markets in 2000	Charles H. Dallara/ Robert Hormats
00-13	Relationship between Corporation and Finance: Current Status and Prospects	Youngkeun Lee
00-14	How Should Korea Cope with Financial Globalization	James P. Rooney

2001

	Title	Author
01-01	The US Economy on the Brink? Japan on the Edge? Implications for Korea	Kenneth S. Courtis
01-02	The Economic Policy of the Bush Administration toward Korea	Marcus Noland

	Title	Author
01-03	Overcoming 3Cs	Jeffrey D. Jones
01-04	High Tech, The Consequences for our Relationship with Technology on our Lives and Businesses	John Naisbitt
01-05	Korea and the IMF	Stanley Fischer
01-06	The Status of Korea's Restructuring: An Outlook over the Next 10 Years	Dominic Barton
01-07	The World Dollar Standard and the East Asian Exchange Rate Dilemma	Ronald McKinnon
01-08	Europe's Role in Global Governance and Challenges to East Asia	Pierre Jacquet

2002

	Title	Author
02-01	Managing Capital Inflows: The Chilean Experience	Carlos Massad
02-02	Globalization and Korea: Opportunities and Backlash and Challenges	Martin Wolf
02-03	The US-Japan Economic Relationship and Implications for Korea	Marcus Noland
02-04	US Global Recovery: For Real? - Prospects and Risks	Allen Sinai
02-05	Globalization: A Force for Good	Patricia Hewitt
02-06	The World after 9/11: A Clash of Civilization?	Francis Fukuyama
02-07	Hanging Together: On Monetary and Financial Cooperation in Asia	Barry Eichengreen
02-08	The Global Economy Rebounds - But How Fast and For How Long? Issues and Implications for Korea and Asia	Kenneth S. Courtis
02-09	The US Economy and the Future of the Dollar: An Outlook for the World Economy	Marcus Noland
02-10	The Doha Round: Objectives, Problems and Prospects	Jagdish Bhagwati
02-11	The Outlook for Korea and the Global Economy 2002-2003	Paul F. Gruenwald
02-12	The US and World Economy: Current Status and Prospects	John B. Taylor
02-13	9/11 and the US Approach to the Korean Peninsula	Thomas C. Hubbard
02-14	The Outlook for US Economy, the Dollar and US Trade Policy	C. Fred Bergsten
02-15	New Challenges and Opportunities for the Global Telecommunications and Information Industries	Peter F. Cowhey

2003

	Title	Author
03-01	The US and World Economy: After the Iraq War	Allen Sinai
03-02	Korea in the OECD Family	Donald Johnston
03-03	The New Role of the US in the Asia-Pacific	Charles Morrison
03-04	The Global Economic Outlook and the Impact of President Bush's Economic Stimulus Package	Phil Gramm
03-05	Europe and Germany in Transition, Where Will the Economies Go?	Hans Tietmeyer
03-06	Regional Financial Cooperation in East Asia	Eisuke Sakakibara
03-07	The Global Exchange Rate Regime and Implications for East Asian Currencies	John Williamson

2004

	Title	Author
04-01	General Outlook on the US and World Economy in 2004	Allen Sinai
04-02	Korea after Kim Jong-il	Marcus Noland
04-03	US-Japan Relations and Implications for Korea	Hugh Patrick/ Gerald Curtis
04-04	China's Economic Rise and New Regional Growth Paradigm	Zhang Yunling
04-05	The Case for a Common Currency in Asia	Robert Mundell
04-06	A Foreign Businessman's Observations on Korean Economy and Other Things	William C. Oberlin

2005

	Title	Author
05-01	US Trade Policy after the 2004 US Election	Peter F. Cowhey
05-02	Asia in Transition and Implications for Korea	Dominic Barton
05-03	Post-Election US and Global Economies: Market Prospects, Risks, and Issues	Allen Sinai
05-04	The Korean Economy: A Critical Assessment from the Japanese Perspective	Yukiko Fukagawa
05-05	The Blind Man and the Elephant: Competing Perspectives on Global Imbalances	Barry Eichengreen
05-06	Mutual Interdependence: Asia and the World Economy	Anne O. Krueger

	Title	Author
05-07	The Impact of China and India on the Global Economy	Wendy Dobson
05-08	Economic Integration between East Asia and Asia-Pacific	Robert Scollay
05-09	Moody's Perspective on Korea's Ratings	Thomas Byrne

2006

	Title	Author
06-01	Oil Prices, Ben Bernanke, Inflation, and the Fourth Energy Recession	Philip K. Verleger
06-02	US and Global Economy and Financial Market Prospects: Picking up Steam	Allen Sinai
06-03	Korea-US FTA: A Path to Sustainable Growth	Alexander Vershbow
06-04	Japan's Foreign Policy for Economy and Japan-Korea FTA	Oshima Shotaro
06-05	Japan's Economic Recovery: Implications for Korea	Yukiko Fukagawa
06-06	M&A in the 21st Century and its Implications	Robert F. Bruner
06-07	Korea's Growing Stature in the Global Economy	Charles H. Dallara
06-08	Asian Economic Integration and Common Asian Currency	Eisuke Sakakibara
06-09	Measuring American Power in Today's Complex World and China "Rising": What Lessons for Today from the Past?	Paul Kennedy/ Bernard Gordon
06-10	- Whither China? - The Global Scramble for IT Leadership: Winners and Losers	- Richard N. Cooper - George Scalise

2007

	Title	Author
07-01	Korea and the United States - Forging a Partnership for the Future: A View from Washington	Edwin J. Feulner
07-02	Germany: Understanding for the Underperformance since Reunification	Juergen B. Donges
07-03	Seismic Shifts, the World Economy, and Financial Markets in 2007	Allen Sinai
07-04	Changing Economic Environment: Their Implications for Korea	Angel Gurría
07-05	The Feasibility of Establishing an East Asian FTA: A Chinese Perspective	Zhang Yunling
07-06	The Global Oil and Gas Market: Paradigm Shift and Implications for Korea	Fereidun Fesharaki

	Title	Author
07-07	The Changing World Economy and Implications for Korea	Anne O. Krueger
07-08	The Longest Recovery of the Japanese Economy: Prospects and Challenges	Yukiko Fukagawa
07-09	Digital Networked Economy and Global Corporate Strategy	Ben Verwaayen
07-10	Moving Forward on the KORUS FTA: Now for the Hard Time	Jeffrey Schott
07-11	The Korean Economy and the FTA with the United States	Barry Eichengreen
07-12	- The Outlook for East Asian Economic Integration: Coping with American Protectionism, Chinese Power, and Japanese Recovery - Economic Outlook for Korea and the Region	- David Hale - Jerald Schiff
07-13	- Why the US Will Continue to Lead the 21st Century? - The Outlook of the Indian Economy from Business Perspective: Implications for Korean Business	- Guy Sorman - Tarun Das

2008

	Title	Author
08-01	Successes of Globalization: the Case of Korea	Anne O. Krueger
08-02	The US "Risk" to Asia and Global Expansion	Allen Sinai
08-03	Europe's Slow Growth: A Warning for Korea	Guy Sorman
08-04	Global Challenges that Will Confront the Next US President	James A. Baker III
08-05	Current Status and Prospects of the Japanese Capital Markets	Atsushi Saito
08-06	Economic and Political Outlook for America and their Implications to the World	Phil Gramm
08-07	The Outlook of the Regional and Global Economic and Financial Situation: Perspectives on International Banking	Charles H. Dallara
08-08	Can South Korea Still Compete?	Guy Sorman
08-09	- Sovereign Wealth Funds: Perceptions and Realities - Global Financial Markets under Stress	- Robert C. Pozen - Jeffrey R. Shafer

2009

	Title	Author
09-01	Global and Regional Economic Developments and Prospects, and the Implications for Korea	Subir Lall
09-02	Competing in an Era of Turbulence and Transition	Deborah Wince-Smith
09-03	US and Global Economic and Financial Crisis: Prospects, Policies, and Perspectives	Allen Sinai
09-04	US Trade Policy in the Obama Era	Jeffrey Schott
09-05	Beyond Keynesianism	Justin Yifu Lin
09-06	- Current Crisis and the Impact on Developing Countries - Lessons from the Current Economic Crisis	- Danny Leipziger - Anne O. Krueger
09-07	- Obama, Can It Work? - The US-Korea Economic Partnership: Working Together in a Time of Global Crisis	- Guy Sorman - Jeffrey Schott

2010

	Title	Author
10-01	The EU in Transition in the New Global Paradigm: Opportunities for Korea	Jean-Pierre Lehmann
10-02	Aftermath of the 'Crises': US and Global Prospects, Legacies, and Policies	Allen Sinai
10-03	The Global Economy: Where Do We Stand?	Anne O. Krueger
10-04	- Japan and Korea in Globalization and its Backlash: Challenges and Prospects - An Overview of China: Economic Prospects and Challenges	- Yukiko Fukagawa - Danny Leipziger
10-05	- Emerging Markets and New Frontiers - Asia in the Global Economy	- Mark Mobius - Dominique Strauss-Kahn
10-06	Rebalancing the World Economy	Paul A. Volcker

2011

	Title	Author
11-01	After the Crisis: What Next in 2011 and 2012?	Allen Sinai
11-02	Safety and Economics of Nuclear Power	SoonHeung Chang
11-03	A Special Lecture on the Rebalancing of the Chinese Economy	Yu Yongding

	Title	Author
11-04	Reshaping the Global Financial Landscape: An Asian Perspective	Institute for Global Economics
11-05	- Economic Outlook and Future Challenges in Developing Asia - Europe's Financial Woes	- Haruhiko Kuroda - Richard N. Cooper
11-06	- Can the G20 Save Globalization and Multilateralism? - Markets, Economic Changes, and Political Stability in North Korea	- Danny Leipziger - Marcus Noland

2012

	Title	Author
12-01	US and Global Economy and Financial Markets in Turmoil: What Lies Ahead?	Allen Sinai
12-02	- Advancement and Education of Science and Technology University and Economic Growth - Prospects of the Eurozone Crisis and its Implications for the Global Economy	- Nam Pyo Suh - Hans Martens
12-03	- The US Elections in 2012 and the Future of US Asia-Pacific Policy - Current Economic Affairs and the Financial Market - An Optimist View on the Global Economy	- Charles Morrison - Charles H. Dallara - Guy Sorman
12-04	- FTAs, Asia-Pacific Integration and Korea - The Eurozone Crisis: Update and Outlook	- Peter A. Petri - Nicolas Véron
12-05	- China's New Leadership and Economic Policy Challenges - Can the WTO Be Resuscitated? Implications for Korea and the Asia Pacific	- Andrew Sheng - Jean-Pierre Lehmann

2013

	Title	Author
13-01	After the Crisis: What Next in 2011 and 2012?	Allen Sinai
13-02	The Eurozone Crisis and its Impact on the Global Economy	Guntram B. Wolff
13-03	- The European Sovereign Debt Crisis: Challenges and How to Solve Them - The Global Outlook: Grounds for Optimism, but Risks Remain Relevant	- Andreas Dombret - John Lipsky
13-04	- The State and Outlook of the US and Chinese Economy - Japan's Abenomics and Foreign Policy	- David Hale - Hugh Patrick/ Gerald Curtis

	Title	Author
13-05	- The Creative Economy and Culture in Korea - Abenomics, Future of the Japanese Economy and the TPP	- Guy Sorman - Yukiko Fukagawa/ Jeffrey Schott
13-06	- Unified Germany in Europe: An Economic Perspective - Chinese Economic Policymaking: A Foreigners' Perspective	- Karl-Heinz Paqué - Bob Davis
13-07	- The Outlook for Japan under Abenomics and Abenationalism - After the Pax Americana (Korea-China-Japan Political and Economic Relation: Whither to?)	- David Asher - David Filling

2014

	Title	Author
14-01	U.S. and Global Economics-Poised for Better Times	- Allen Sinai
14-02	- Abe in the Driver's Seat: Where is the Road Leading? - The Secret of Germany's Performance: The Mittelstand Economy	- Gerald Curtis - Peter Friedrich
14-03	- The Eurozone Economy: Out of the Doldrums? - The Globla Economy 2014	- Karl-Heinz Paqué - Martin Feldstein
14-04	Philanthropy and Welfare	- Guy Sorman
14-05	- Global Trade Environment and the Future of the World Economy - From BRICs to America	- Roberto Azevêdo - Sung Won Sohn
14-06	- Risks and Opportunities in the Global Economic Recovery - Abe's Labor Reform and Innovative Strategies	- Charles H. Dallara - Yukiko Fukagawa
14-07	- China's Economy and Anti-Corruption Drive - US Fed's QE Ending & Asian Financial Markets - China's New Economic Strategies and the Korea-China FTA	- Bob Davis - Anoop Singh - Zhang Yunling

2015

	Title	Author
15-01	- Will the Global Economy Normalize in 2015?	- Allen Sinai
15-02	- The EU Economy in 2015: Will It Take Off? - U.S.-Korea Economic Relations: Partnership for Shared Economic Prosperity - The Hartz Labor Reforms of Germany and the Implications for Korea	- Jeroen Dijsselbloem - Mark W. Lippert - Peter Hartz
15-03	- What Makes China Grow? - What can Korea Learn from Europe's Slow Growth?	- Lawrence Lau - Guy Sorman

	Title	Author
15-04	- Global Energy and Environmental Issues and Switzerland - The Emerging New Asian Economic Disorder	- H.E. Doris Leuthard - David L. Asher
15-05	- The Chinese Economy: Transition towards the New Normal - Germany's Industry 4.0: Harnessing the Potential of Digitization	- Huang Yiping - Matthias Machnig
15-06	- Four Global Forces Changing the World - Turbulence in Emerging Markets and Impact on Korea	- Dominic Barton - Sung-won Sohn
15-07	- Observations on the Korean Economy and North Korea's Economic Potential - Perspectives on China's Economy and Economic Reform	- Thomas Byrne - Huang Haizhou

2016

	Title	Author
16-01	- The U.S. and Global Prospects and Markets in 2016: A Look Ahead	- Allen Sinai
16-02	- The Key Themes and Risks of the Global Economy in 2016 - The U.S. in the Global Economy	- Hung Tran - Anne Krueger
16-03	- The Prospects and Impact of the U.S. Election and Economy - The US and Northeast Asia in a Turbulent Time	- Martin Feldstein - Gerald Curtis
16-04	- The U.S. Presidential Election and Its Economic and Security Implications - The World Economy at a Time of Monetary Experimentation and Political Fracture - Allies in Business: The Future of the U.S.-ROK Economic Relationship	- Marcus Noland & Sung-won Sohn - Charles H. Dallara - Mark Lippert

2017

	Title	Author
17-01	- Big Changes, Big Effects - U.S. and Global Economic and Financial Prospects 2017	- Allen Sinai
17-02	- The 2017 US and Global Macroeconomic Outlook - Automation, Jobs and the Future of Work in Korea	- Martin Feldstein - Jonathan Woetzel
17-03	- Trump's US, Japan's Economy and Korea - Between Brexit and Trump: Global Challenges for the European Union	- Gerald Curtis & Hugh Paztrick - Thomas Wieser
17-04	- The Future of Work: Is This Time Different?	- Carl Benedikt Frey

	Title	Author
17-05	- The Future of Growth - The Current State of US Economy and Trump Administration's Trade Policy with Special Reference to the KORUS FTA Revision	- Simon Baptist - Sung-won Sohn & Jeffrey Schott

2018

	Title	Author
18-01	- Dr. Martin Feldstein's Analysis of the US and Global Economy - U.S. and Global Prospects Looking Ahead	- Martin Feldstein - Allen Sinai
18-02	- US Protectionism, China's Political Shift and Their Implications - Japan's Labor Reform and Future Korea-Japan Cooperation	- Kenneth Courtis - Yukiko Fukagawa
18-03	- U.S. Economic and Trade Policy for Korea and Asia - How Europeans See China, Changing World Order and Its Implications for Korea	- Charles Freeman - Guy Sorman
18-04	- Asia's New Economic Landscape: India, Japan and China - Climate, Energy and Green Tech: Transforming Our Economies	- Eisuke Sakakibara - Karsten Sach

2019

	Title	Author
19-01	- Financial Innovation, FinTech and the Future of Finance - Setting up Canada's National Pension System for Success – CPPIB's Perspectives	- Robert Merton - Suyi Kim
19-02	- Why I Remain Optimistic about China: Why China's Worst Enemy in the Short-Term Will Prove its Best Friend in the Long-Term - The World in 2019: U.S., Global Economies, Policies and Markets – Can Expansion be sustained?	- Henny Sender - Allen Sinai
19-03	- A Brief Tour of Global Near-term Risks and Long-run Concerns about the International Financial Architecture - 5 Ways the Financial System Will Fail Next Time	-Carmen Reinhart -Michael Barr
19-04	- Beyond 1980's: The New Horizon of Japan-Korea Economic Relations - Reflections on the Japanese Economy and Abenomics	-Yukiko Fukagawa -Hugh Patrick
19-05	- Financial Innovation and Asset Management Strategies in the Age of Hyper-Low Interest Rates	- Robert Merton
19-06	- Artificial Intelligence (AI) and its Impact on the Future of Economy and Society - U.S.-China, Korea-Japan Trade Disputes and the Global Trading System	- Jerome Glenn - Jeffrey Schott

		Title	Author
19-10	Oct 22	Financial Innovation and Asset Management Strategies in the Age of Hyper−Low Interest Rates	Robert Merton
19-11	Nov 19	Artificial Intelligence (AI) and its Impact on the Future of Economy and Society	Jerome Glenn

2020

		Title	Author
20-01	Jan 16	Charting 'Uncharted Waters': The U.S. and World in 2020	Allen Sinai
20-02	May 28	The 30th Anniversary of the German Reunification: Lessons and Policy Implications	Stephan Auer

2021

	Title	Author
21-01	- Geopolitical Challenges and Opportunities in East Asia Under the Biden Administration - Emerging Trends and Issues for International Capital Markets and BlackRock's ESG Strategy - 2021 Global and Asia Pacific Regional Economic Outlook - Prospects for the U.S. and Global Economies and Financial Markets in 2021	- Evans J.R. Revere - Henny Sender - Shaun Roache - Allen Sinai
21-02	- Biden Administration's Foreign Policy on Asia: Prospects for US-China Relations and Implications for Korea - The Future of International Trading System under the Biden Administration and Its Implications for Korea: Whither US Commercial Policy toward Asia?	- Victor Cha - Jeffrey J. Schott

2022

	Title	Author
22-01	- The Future of Cryptocurrency - Perspectives on ESG Investing from CPP Investments & Prospects for International Financial Markets - China's Economy at a Crossroads: Implications for US-China Relations and Korea	- Brian Brooks - Suyi Kim - David Dollar
22-02	- 2022 Prospects for Global Economy and Trade, and Implications for Korea - Geopolitical Risk Proliferation and Role of the ROK-US Alliance: Policy Implications for the New Korean administration - New Challenges for World Trade after Russia's Invasion of Ukraine	- Anne Krueger - Victor Cha - Jeffrey J. Schott

2023

	Title	Author
23-01	- Navigating the Global Multiple Economic Crises: Geopolitical and Policy Implications for Korea - US-Korea Alliance: New Challenges, New Strength - Supply Chain Crisis: Myths and Realities - Global Financial Market Turmoil Emergency Check: Asia, are we going under again?	- Charles H. Dallara - Evans J.R. Revere - Robert Dohner - Tai Hui
23-02	- The Future of US-China Decoupling Amid Weakening Chinese Economic Prospects - S.Korea diplomatic and security policy review and Implications for cooperation with US & Japan - US-China Conflict: A New Roadmap to Restoring Mutually Advantageous Relationship - 2023 Global Economic Prospects and the Challenges for Korea	- Nicholas R. Lardy - Victor Cha - Stephen Roach - Robert Subbaraman

2024

	Title	Author
24-01	- The Bitcoin Spot ETF and Its Implications for the Future of Finance - The Road Ahead: Key Global Geopolitical Challenges and Path Forward to 2024 - 2024 Global Trade and East Asia Economy Outlook: The Future of Korea-Japan Cooperation	- Brian Brooks - Gi-Wook Shin - Fukagawa Yukiko

2025

	Title	Author
25-01	Korea's Political and Security Crisis: U.S.-ROK Alliance and North Korea Strategy under Trump 2.0	Victor Cha
25-02	Enhancing Korea's International Competitiveness: The Role of Finance in Times of Crisis	Michael Mainelli

세계경제연구원 간행물

Occasional Paper Series

1993

연 번	제 목	저 자
93-01	Clintonomics and the New World Order: Implications for Korea-US Relations	C. Fred Bergsten
93-02	The Uruguay Round, NAFTA, and US-Korea Economic Relations	Jeffrey Schott

1994

연 번	제 목	저 자
94-01	21세기 준비 어떻게 할 것인가	Paul Kennedy
94-02	미국과 일본 간의 기술경쟁과 한국에 미칠 영향	Ronald A. Morse
94-03	일본경제, 무엇이 문제인가	Toyoo Gyohten
94-04	미국경제와 세계경제: 현황과 전망	Allen Sinai
94-05	국제환율제도 이대로 좋은가	John Williamson
94-06	The Promises of the WTO for the Trading Community	Arthur Dunkel

1995

연 번	제 목	저 자
95-01	멕시코 페소화 위기와 세계금융시장 동향	Charles H. Dallara
95-02	세계경제 동향과 미국경제 전망	Allen Sinai
95-03	새로운 게임, 새로운 규칙과 새로운 전략	Lester Thurow
95-04	미국·북한관계 전망	Robert Scalapino
95-05	미국의 동아시아 정책과 한반도	James A. Baker III
95-06	미일 무역마찰과 한국	Anne O. Krueger
95-07	동북아경제권 개발 전망: 일본의 시각	Hisao Kanamori

1996

연 번	제 목	저 자
96-01	Trends of International Financial Market and Prospects of Global Economy in 1996	Allen Sinai
96-02	유럽연합(EU)의 앞날과 세계경제	Jørgen Ørstrøm Møller
96-03	세계경제와 OECD의 역할	Donald Johnston
96-04	동아시아 경제성장의 정치적 배경과 영향	Francis Fukuyama

연 번	제 목	저 자
96-05	국제사회에서의 한국의 새 역할	A. W. Clausen

1997

연 번	제 목	저 자
97-01	다국적기업과 동아시아 경제통합	Wendy Dobson
97-02	아태 지역에 대한 미국의 안보정책	William J. Perry
97-03	뉴질랜드의 공공부문 개혁	Donald Hunn

1998

연 번	제 목	저 자
98-01	범세계적 기업과 다자간 투자협정	Edward M. Graham
98-02	변화 속의 안정: 새로운 한미 관계의 모색	W. Anthony Lake
98-03	한국: 동북아의 새로운 협력 중심으로	Donald P. Gregg
98-04	경제적 측면에서 본 독일 통일의 교훈	Juergen B. Donges
98-05	세계화와 종족화: 20세기 말의 딜레마	Guy Sorman

1999

연 번	제 목	저 자
99-01	북한의 정치·경제 상황과 동북아 안보	Marcus Noland
99-02	엔-달러 환율과 국제금융시장	Kenneth S. Courtis
99-03	한국과 아시아 경제: 전망과 정책대응	Donald Johnston/ Hubert Neiss
99-04	미국과 일본경제의 비교평가	Hugh Patrick
99-05	세계경제: 도전과 전망	Rudiger Dornbusch

2000

연 번	제 목	저 자
00-01	한미관계: 번영과 안보의 동반자	Stephen W. Bosworth
00-02	글로벌 뉴 이코노미: 도전과 한국의 활로	양수길
00-03	금융감독의 세계적 조류	이용근
00-04	성장하는 아시아와 침체 속의 일본	Kenneth S. Courtis
00-05	세계금융체제의 미래와 우리의 대응	Morris Goldstein
00-06	시애틀 이후의 WTO와 한미FTA전망	Jeffrey Schott/ 최인범
00-07	다자간 국제경제기구의 미래와 전망	Anne O. Krueger
00-08	남북한 관계: 현황과 전망	Marcus Noland

연 번	제 목	저 자
00-09	Knowledge 시대의 외국인 직접투자 유치	Andrew Fraser
00-10	미국 新행정부 및 의회의 대외·경제정책방향	C. Fred Bergsten
00-11	한미관계: 번영과 안보의 동반자	Stephen W. Bosworth
00-12	2000년 국제금융 및 신흥시장 전망	Charles H. Dallara/ Robert Hormats
00-13	기업·금융 관계: 현황과 전망	이용근
00-14	금융세계화, 어떻게 대처하나	James P. Rooney

2001

연 번	제 목	저 자
01-01	2001년 미국, 일본경제와 아시아	Kenneth S. Courtis
01-02	부시행정부의 對韓 경제정책과 한국의 대응	Marcus Noland
01-03	3C를 극복하자	Jeffrey D. Jones
01-04	하이테크와 비즈니스, 그리고 세계경제	John Naisbitt
01-05	한국과 IMF	Stanley Fischer
01-06	한국경제의 향후 10년	Dominic Barton
01-07	세계 달러본위제도와 동아시아 환율딜레마	Ronald McKinnon
01-08	新국제질서 속의 유럽과 한국	Pierre Jacquet

2002

연 번	제 목	저 자
02-01	금융위기 再發 어떻게 막나: 칠레의 경험을 중심으로	Carlos Massad
02-02	세계경제의 기회와 위험	Martin Wolf
02-03	美·日 경제현황과 한국의 대응	Marcus Noland
02-04	미국경제와 세계경제: 회복가능성과 위험	Allen Sinai
02-05	세계화: 혜택의 원동력	Patricia Hewitt
02-06	9·11테러사태 이후의 세계질서: 문명의 충돌인가?	Francis Fukuyama
02-07	아시아지역의 통화·금융 협력	Barry Eichengreen
02-08	세계경제, 회복되나?	Kenneth S. Courtis
02-09	미국경제와 달러의 장래	Marcus Noland
02-10	도하라운드: 문제점과 전망	Jagdish Bhagwati
02-11	2003 한국경제와 세계경제 전망	Paul F. Gruenwald
02-12	미국경제 현황과 세계경제의 앞날	John B. Taylor
02-13	9·11사태와 미국의 한반도정책	Thomas C. Hubbard
02-14	미국 경제, 달러 및 대외통상정책 방향	C. Fred Bergsten
02-15	미국의 IT산업 관련 정책과 한국	Peter F. Cowhey

2003

연 번	제 목	저 자
03-01	이라크전 이후의 미국경제와 세계경제	Allen Sinai
03-02	OECD가 본 한국경제	Donald Johnston
03-03	아태 지역에서의 미국의 새 역할	Charles Morrison
03-04	세계경제 전망과 부시행정부의 경기부양책	Phil Gramm
03-05	침체된 독일・유럽 경제가 주는 정책적 교훈과 시사	Hans Tietmeyer
03-06	동아시아 금융협력과 한국	Eisuke Sakakibara
03-07	세계환율체제 개편과 동아시아 경제	John Williamson

2004

연 번	제 목	저 자
04-01	2004 미국경제와 세계경제 전망	Allen Sinai
04-02	김정일 이후의 한반도	Marcus Noland
04-03	미국 대통령 선거와 韓・美・日관계	Hugh Patrick/ Gerald Curtis
04-04	중국경제의 부상과 동북아 지역경제	Zhang Yunling
04-05	아시아 화폐단일화, 가능한가?	Robert Mundell
04-06	외국기업인의 눈에 비친 한국경제	William C. Oberlin

2005

연 번	제 목	저 자
05-01	대통령선거 이후의 미국 통상정책, 어떻게 되나	Peter F. Cowhey
05-02	아시아 경제・무역환경, 어떻게 전개되나?	Dominic Barton
05-03	제2기 부시 행정부의 경제정책과 세계경제 및 시장 전망	Allen Sinai
05-04	일본의 시각에서 본 한국경제의 활로	Yukiko Fukagawa
05-05	세계경제, 무엇이 문제인가	Barry Eichengreen
05-06	세계 속의 한국경제: 역할과 전망	Anne O. Krueger
05-07	중국과 인도가 세계경제에 미치는 영향	Wendy Dobson
05-08	동아시아와 아태지역 경제통합	Robert Scollay
05-09	국제신용평가기관이 보는 한국	Thomas Byrne

2006

연 번	제 목	저 자
06-01	고유가와 세계경제의 앞날	Philip K. Verleger
06-02	2006년 미국경제/세계경제와 금융시장 전망	Allen Sinai

연 번	제 목	저 자
06-03	한미FTA: 지속성장의 활로	Alexander Vershbow
06-04	일본의 대외경제정책과 한일 FTA	Oshima Shotaro
06-05	일본경제 회생과 한국경제	Yukiko Fukagawa
06-06	세계 M&A시장 현황과 전망: 우리의 대응	Robert F. Bruner
06-07	세계인이 보는 한국경제는?	Charles H. Dallara
06-08	아시아 공통통화와 아시아 경제통합	Eisuke Sakakibara
06-09	미국의 힘은 얼마나 강하며, 중국의 부상은 어떻게 보아야 하는가?	Paul Kennedy/ Bernard Gordon
06-10	- 20년 후의 중국, 어떤 모습일까? - 세계 IT 리더십 경쟁: 승자와 패자	- Richard N. Cooper - George Scalise

2007

연 번	제 목	저 자
07-01	한미관계: 새로운 동반자 시대를 지향하며	Edwin J. Feulner
07-02	통일 이후 독일: 경제침체의 교훈	Juergen B. Donges
07-03	2007년 세계경제와 금융시장의 지각변동	Allen Sinai
07-04	급변하는 세계경제환경, 어떻게 대처해야 하나	Angel Gurría
07-05	동아시아 FTA 가능한가?: 중국의 시각	Zhang Yunling
07-06	구조적 변화 맞고 있는 세계석유시장과 한국	Fereidun Fesharaki
07-07	변모하는 세계경제와 한국	Anne O. Krueger
07-08	되살아나는 일본경제: 전망과 과제	Yukiko Fukagawa
07-09	디지털 네트워크 경제와 글로벌 기업 전략	Ben Verwaayen
07-10	한미FTA: 미국의 시각	Jeffrey Schott
07-11	한미FTA와 한국경제의 미래	Barry Eichengreen
07-12	- 동아시아 경제통합, 어떻게 보나 - 한국경제 및 동아시아경제 전망	- David Hale - Jerald Schiff
07-13	- 21세기는 여전히 미국의 세기가 될 것인가? - 인도경제 전망과 한국 기업	- Guy Sorman - Tarun Das

2008

연 번	제 목	저 자
08-01	국가 미래를 위한 한국의 세계화 전략	Anne O. Krueger
08-02	2008년 미국경제와 세계금융시장 동향	Allen Sinai
08-03	유럽의 경제침체: 우리에게 주는 시사점	Guy Sorman
08-04	차기 미국 대통령이 풀어야할 세계적 도전	James A. Baker III
08-05	일본 자본시장의 현재와 전망	Atsushi Saito

연 번	제 목	저 자
08-06	대선 이후 미국의 정치·경제, 어떻게 전개되나?	Phil Gramm
08-07	세계 및 아시아 경제·금융 전망	Charles H. Dallara
08-08	한국경제의 경쟁력 강화, 어떻게 하나?	Guy Sorman
08-09	- 국부펀드: 인식과 현실 - 긴장 속의 세계금융시장, 어떻게 되나?	- Robert C. Pozen - Jeffrey R. Shafer

2009

연 번	제 목	저 자
09-01	2009년 한국경제와 세계 및 아시아 경제 전망	Subir Lall
09-02	혼란과 전환기의 경쟁력 강화: 과제와 전망	Deborah Wince-Smith
09-03	위기 속의 미국 및 세계 경제와 금융: 전망과 정책대응	Allen Sinai
09-04	미국 오바마 행정부의 통상정책	Jeffrey Schott
09-05	하강하는 세계경제와 케인지언 정책 처방의 실효성	Justin Yifu Lin
09-06	- 세계금융위기가 개도국에 미치는 여파와 대응 - 최근 세계경제위기의 교훈과 전망	- Danny Leipziger - Anne O. Krueger
09-07	- 미국 오바마 행정부의 경제 및 대외정책, 어떻게 되나? - 한미 경제 파트너십: 세계적 위기에 어떻게 협력할 것인가	- Guy Sorman - Jeffrey Schott

2010

연 번	제 목	저 자
10-01	새로운 세계질서 속에 변화하는 EU: 한국의 기회는?	Jean-Pierre Lehmann
10-02	위기 이후 미국 및 세계경제 전망, 그리고 유산과 정책 과제	Allen Sinai
10-03	세계경제, 어떻게 볼 것인가?: 진단과 전망	Anne O. Krueger
10-04	- 세계화 파고 속의 한국과 일본경제: 도전과 전망 - 중국 경제의 虛와 實	- Yukiko Fukagawa - Danny Leipziger
10-05	- 신흥국 자본시장과 뉴 프런티어 - 세계경제와 아시아의 역할	- Mark Mobius - Dominique Strauss-Kahn
10-06	세계경제의 재균형	Paul A. Volcker

2011

연 번	제 목	저 자
11-01	위기 이후의 세계경제와 한국경제: 2011년 및 2012년 전망	Allen Sinai
11-02	원자력 발전의 안전성과 경제성: 한국의 선택은?	장순흥
11-03	중국 경제의 재(再)균형	Yu Yongding
11-04	세계금융질서의 개편: 아시아의 시각	세계경제연구원
11-05	- 아시아 경제의 발전전망과 도전과제 - 유럽의 국가채무위기: 평가와 전망	- Haruhiko Kuroda - Richard N. Cooper
11-06	- 기로에 선 세계화와 다자주의, 그리고 G-20 - 북한의 시장과 경제, 그리고 정치적 안정성, 어떻게 변화하고 있나?	- Danny Leipziger - Marcus Noland

2012

연 번	제 목	저 자
12-01	혼돈 속의 세계경제와 금융시장: 분석과 2012년 전망	Allen Sinai
12-02	- 카이스트의 혁신 - 유로위기 해결책은 없나	- 서남표 - Hans Martens
12-03	- 2012년 미국의 대선과 향후 아태정책 전망 - 세계경제 및 금융시장 현황 - 그래도 세계경제의 미래는 밝다	- Charles Morrison - Charles H. Dallara - Guy Sorman
12-04	- FTA와 아태지역 통합 그리고 한국 - 유로위기 언제 끝나나?	- Peter A. Petri - Nicolas Véron
12-05	- 중국의 새 리더십과 경제정책 - 국제통상질서의 현황과 WTO의 미래	- Andrew Sheng - Jean-Pierre Lehmann

2013

연 번	제 목	저 자
13-01	2013년 세계경제와 미국경제 전망	Allen Sinai
13-02	유로존, 올해는 위기에서 벗어날 수 있나?	Guntram B. Wolff
13-03	- 유럽국채위기: 과제와 해결책 - 세계경제, 언제 회복되나?	- Andreas Dombret - John Lipsky
13-04	- 미국과 중국경제 현황과 전망 - 일본의 아베노믹스와 외교정책	- David Hale - Hugh Patrick/Gerald Curtis
13-05	- 한국의 창조경제와 문화 - 아베노믹스와 일본 경제의 미래, 그리고 TPP	- Guy Sorman - Yukiko Fukagawa/ Jeffrey Schott
13-06	- 통일 독일의 경제·정치적 위상: 한국에 대한 시사점 - 외국인이 바라본 중국의 경제정책	- Karl-Heinz Paqué - Bob Davis

2014

연번	제 목	저 자
14-01	2014년 세계경제, 나아질 것인가?	Allen Sinai
14-02	- 아베정권은 어디로 가고 있나? - 중견기업: 순항하는 독일경제의 비결	- Gerald Curtis - Peter Friedrich
14-03	- 유럽경제, 살아날 것인가? - 2014년 세계 경제의 향방은?	- Karl-Heinz Paqué - Martin Feldstein
14-04	복지향상과 기부문화	Guy Sorman
14-05	- 세계무역 환경과 세계경제의 미래 - 브릭스(BRICs)에서 미국으로	- Roberto Azevêdo - Sung Won Sohn
14-06	- 세계경제 회복, 위기인가 기회인가 - 아베 정권의 노동개혁과 혁신전략은 성공할 것인가	- Charles H. Dallara - Yukiko Fukagawa
14-07	- 중국경제 현황과 시진핑의 반부패운동 - 다가올 미 연준의 QE종료가 아시아 금융시장에 미칠 영향 - 중국의 신경제 전략과 한-중 FTA	- Bob Davis - Anoop Singh - Zhang Yunling

2015

연번	제 목	저 자
15-01	2015년 세계경제, 정상화될 것인가	Allen Sinai
15-02	- 2015년 유럽경제, 회복될 것인가? - 공동 번영을 위한 한미 경제 파트너십 - 독일 하르츠 노동개혁과 한국에 대한 시사점	- Jeroen Dijsselbloem - Mark W. Lippert - Peter Hartz
15-03	- 중국 경제의 앞날을 내다보며 - 유럽의 저성장에서 우리는 무엇을 배워야 하는가?	- Lawrence Lau - Guy Sorman
15-04	- 글로벌 에너지(중점)환경 이슈와 스위스의 경험 - 혼돈의 아시아 경제, 어디로 가는가	- H.E. Doris Leuthard - David L. Asher
15-05	- 중국 경제의 신창타이(新常態)는 무엇인가 - 디지털화를 활용한 독일의 산업혁명 4.0	- Huang Yiping - Matthias Machnig
15-06	- 세상을 바꾸는 네 가지 글로벌 흐름 - 격변하는 신흥시장과 한국에 미칠 영향	- Dominic Barton - Sung-won Sohn
15-07	- 내가 본 한국, 한국 경제, 그리고 북한 경제의 잠재력 - 중국의 경제개혁과 향후 전망	- Thomas Byrne - Huang Haizhou

2016

연번	제 목	저 자
16-01	2016년 세계경제 및 금융시장 전망	- Allen Sinai
16-02	- 2016년 세계 경제의 주요 이슈와 리스크 - 미국의 경제·정치 상황이 세계 경제에 미치는 영향	- Hung Tran - Anne Krueger
16-03	- 미국 경제와 대선이 세계 경제에 미칠 영향 - 미국 대통령 선거가 동북아에 미칠 지정학적 영향과 전망	- Martin Feldstein - Gerald Curtis

연 번	제 목	저 자
16-04	- 미국 새 행정부의 경제와 안보 정책 - 통화정책 실험과 정치 분열기의 세계 경제 - 한미 경제 협력: 현황과 전망	- Marcus Noland & Sung-won Sohn - Charles H. Dallara - Mark Lippert

2017

연 번	제 목	저 자
17-01	- 대변혁 속의 2017 - 미국과 세계 경제 금융 전망	- Allen Sinai
17-02	- 미국 신정부의 경제정책과 2017년 미국 및 세계 경제 전망 - 4차 산업혁명 시대 자동화, 일자리, 그리고 직업의 미래	- Martin Feldstein - Jonathan Woetzel
17-03	- 트럼프의 미국, 일본 경제 그리고 한국 - 브렉시트와 미국의 트럼프 대통령: 유럽의 도전	- Gerald Curtis & Hugh Patrick - Thomas Wieser
17-04	- 직업의 미래 - 이번엔 다른가	- Carl Benedikt Frey
17-05	- 세계경제 성장 전망과 기술의 역할 - 미국경제 현황과 트럼프 행정부의 통상정책 및 한미 FTA 개정	- Simon Baptist - Sung-won Sohn &Jeffrey Schott

2018

연 번	제 목	저 자
18-01	- 펠드스타인 교수가 진단하는 미국과 세계경제 - 2018년 미국과 세계 경제·금융 전망	- Martin Feldstein - Allen Sinai
18-02	- 미국 보호주의와 중국 정치체제 변화의 함의 - 일본 노동개혁과 한일 협력의 미래	- Kenneth Courtis - Yukiko Fukagawa
18-03	- 트럼프 행정부의 한국 및 대아시아 무역·경제 정책 - 유럽이 보는 시진핑 체제하의 중국과 세계 질서	- Charles Freeman - Guy Sorman
18-04	- 새로운 아시아 경제 지평: 일본, 중국 그리고 인도 - 독일의 기후변화, 에너지 및 녹색기술 정책 경험과 한국에 대한 시사점	- Eisuke Sakakibara - Karsten Sach

2019

연 번	제 목	저 자
19-01	- 금융혁신, 핀테크 그리고 금융의 미래 - 캐나다 국민연금 시스템의 성공과 CPPIB	- Robert Merton - Suyi Kim
19-02	- 내가 중국 경제를 여전히 낙관하는 이유: 왜 중국의 단기적 악재가 장기적 호재일까 - 2019년 세계 경제 및 금융 전망 - 과연 경기 확장세는 지속될 것인가?	- Henny Sender - Allen Sinai

연 번	제 목	저 자
19-03	국제금융체제의 단기 리스크와 구조적 문제 향후 금융시스템 실패의 5가지 시나리오	-Carmen Reinhart -Michael Barr
19-04	한 · 일 무역갈등을 넘어서: 양국 경제관계의 새로운 지평 휴 패트릭 교수가 본 일본경제와 아베노믹스	-Yukiko Fukagawa -Hugh Patrick
19-05	초저금리 시대의 금융 혁신과 자산운용 전략	-Robert Merton
19-06	인공지능(AI)이 만드는 경제 · 사회의 미래 미 · 중, 한 · 일 무역분쟁과 세계무역체제	- Jerome Glenn - Jeffrey Schott

2020

연 번	제 목	저 자
20-01	2020년 미국 및 세계 경제 전망: '미지의 바다' 항해도 그리기 −10개의 메시지와 코로나바이러스 충격	- Allen Sinai
20-02	독일 통일 30년의 경험: 교훈과 정책적 시사점	- Stephan Auer

2021

연 번	제 목	저 자
21-01	− 美 바이든 행정부 출범과 동아시아의 지정학적 도전 및 기회 − 국제금융시장 현황 및 핵심 이슈와 블랙록 ESG투자 전략 − 2021 글로벌 경제 전망: 중국 · 일본 · 한국, 아시아 경제의 향방 − 2021년 미국 및 세계 경제 예측과 금융시장 전망	- Evans J.R. Revere - Henny Sender - Shaun Roache - Allen Sinai
21-02	− 바이든 행정부의 아시아 외교정책: 미 · 중 관계 전망과 한국에 대한 시사점 − 바이든 행정부 출범과 국제통상체제의 미래: 미국의 對아시아 통상전략 향방 및 한국에의 시사점	- Victor Cha - Jeffrey J. Schott

2022

연 번	제 목	저 자
22-01	− 가상화폐의 미래 − 캐나다 연기금(CPP)의 ESG 투자 전략과 국제금융시장 전망 − 전환점에 선 중국 경제: 美 中 역학관계와 한국에의 시사점	- Brian Brooks - Suyi Kim - David Dollar
22-02	− 2022년 글로벌 경제 및 무역 전망: 한국에의 정책적 시사점 − 지정학적 리스크 확산과 한미동맹의 역할: 新 정부 외교 안보 전략 시사점 − 러시아의 우크라이나 침공 이후 세계 무역의 새로운 도전	- Anne Krueger - Victor Cha - Jeffrey J. Schott

2023

연 번	제 목	저 자
23-01	– 글로벌 복합 경제 위기 진단: 한국 경제에의 지정학적 및 정책적 시사점 – 한미동맹의 미래: 새로운 도전, 새로운 기회 – 글로벌 공급망 이슈 진단과 세계 경제안보 전망 – 국제 금융시장 긴급진단 웨비나: 달러 초강세 속 亞 외환위기 재발 위험 진단	- Charles H. Dallara - Evans J.R. Revere - Robert Dohner - Tai Hui
23-02	– 중국경제 둔화 전망과 미중 디커플링의 전략적 함의 – 尹정부 1년 외교안보정책 리뷰 및 한미일 공조를 위한 제언 – 美中 패권 갈등: 互惠 관계 회복을 위한 새로운 로드맵 – 2023년 세계경제 전망과 한국경제의 도전	- Nicholas R. Lardy - Victor Cha - Stephen Roach - Robert Subbaraman

2024

연 번	제 목	저 자
24-01	– 비트코인 현물 ETF 등장: 금융투자 게임체인저 되나 – 글로벌 지정학 위기 진단과 2024년 전망 및 시사점 – 2024년 글로벌 무역과 동아시아 경제 전망: 한일 협력의 미래	- Brian Brooks - Gi-Wook Shin - Fukagawa Yukiko

2025

연 번	제 목	저 자
25-01	한국 정치·안보 위기 긴급 진단: 트럼프 2.0 한미동맹의 미래와 대북전략 변화	Victor Cha
25-02	한국의 국제 신인도 제고와 국가 경쟁력 강화를 위한 전략: 금융의 역할	Michael Mainelli